DRAGONS AND POWER

Also by Wendy Palmer

Book: *Leadership Embodiment*
How the Way We Sit and Stand Can Change the Way We Think and
Speak (with co-author, Janet Crawford)
Createspace, An Amazon Company
Publication: 2013

Book: *The Practice of Freedom*
Aikido Principles as a Spiritual Guide
Rodmell Press
Publication: 2000

Book: *The Intuitive Body*
Discovering the Wisdom of Conscious Embodiment and Aikido
North Atlantic Books
Publication dates: 1994, 1999, 2008

DRAGONS AND POWER

*Embodying Your
Noble, Awesome and Shiny
Dragon Spirit*

Wendy Palmer

For information, contact Leadership Embodiment
http://leadershipembodiment.com

Content Editor: Janis Chan
Cover Art: John Lund http://www.johnlund.com
Cover Design: Colleen Dwire http://www.colleendwire.com
Illustrations: Cian Geraghty
Photo of Wendy Palmer: Nick Aldridge

First Edition / Spring 2020

Publisher: Leadership Embodiment

Printed by KDP Publishing, An Amazon Company

ISBN-13: 978-1-7348557-1-5

Library of Congress Control Number: 2020908639

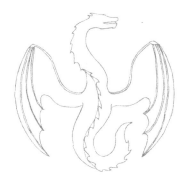

Dedicated to The Mystery
– mother of all Dragons

If you ignore the dragon, it will eat you.

If you try to confront the dragon it will overpower you.

If you ride the dragon, you will take advantage of its might and power.

Chinese Proverb

PRAISE FOR DRAGONS AND POWER

In an era rife with use of power that is either unskillful or just confused, this pithy and potent book offers an immediately accessible way of practicing with ourselves that is direct, compassionate and confident.

Dragons and Power puts a master teacher in your pocket with Wendy Palmer's extensive experience and deep intuition commingling to express wisdom that works for these times: honest, engaging, and straight to – and from – the heart.

— Rev. angel Kyodo williams, Sensei
Author, Radical Dharma Talking Race Love & Liberation

This book is a brilliant guide to embodying body, heart, and mind in the service of inspired creativity, wise compassion and awakened leadership. It's a traveling aikido mat you can take with you to the boardroom or your living room to meet life's challenges with flexibility, courage, and clarity.

–Frank Ostaseski, Author of The Five Invitations: Discovering What Death Can Teach Us About Living Fully

Wendy Palmer is a small woman with a large spirit – and she knows her dragons. This book is a playful, powerful, and practical guide for entering [tapping into] flow and enlarging your leadership presence. Read it, do the tiny practices, and climb on for the ride.

—Mette Norgaard, Ph.D
Founder Strategic Leadership & Learning
New York Times bestselling author of TouchPoints

Equal parts mastery and mystery, Dragon Power presents profound and actionable practices to help us synchronize body and mind, enabling us to embody our true leadership power to help others. Seeing the Big Picture of interconnection is our natural inheritance as human beings; we've all been moved and awed and in flow. In this book, Wendy Palmer takes us by the wrist and shows us how to stabilize this in everyday life.

—James Gimian, Executive Director, Foundation for a Mindful Society

Wendy is widely beloved for her powerful presence — at once fierce and compassionate, focused and open, confident and curious. Over the years, I've personally benefited from Wendy's teachings, as have so many people in my life and work. I am amazed at Wendy's ability to convey her simple, deeply empowering practices in this rich and wonderful narrative. Wendy encourages all of us to source and embrace our full selves and to reap the benefits ... anytime, anywhere.

—Eileen Fisher, founder, EILEEN FISHER, Inc.

CONTENTS

INTRODUCTION

An Experience of Power

I stand in the middle of the Aikido mat. A man half my age and twice my size moves toward me. His right fist is ready, and he lashes out when he is within reach of my face. "Open up", I tell myself, "include him – look into the space."

As the punch whistles past my face, I gently place my hand on his arm for one second, then draw it close to me and pivot for the throw. He flies through the air, lands gracefully and quickly stands ready to strike again.

"Don't think," I tell myself "Just open, keep including him, concentrate on the space, the space will absorb his blow."

This time my hand has some tension as it touches his arm. He tenses, and suddenly we are both tightening our muscles. He whirls around for another punch, and I have to duck. I get the throw off, but it is not smooth and graceful like the first one.

I stop and turn to the students sitting in a line on the mat. "That's what happens when you tense up – your partner will reflect your tension and tense up as well, and then you will be fighting rather than flowing. Cultivate the strength of an uplifted posture and softness in your touch. Open up and include your partner, invite him into your space. Practice with the attitude that you are connected. Together you can flow in the beautiful movement of the technique."

I have experienced moments on the Aikido mat that can only be described as mystical. Moments when the interactions seemed to be in slow motion and I had the sensation of floating in warm space. Time and space morph into a dance of waves and spirals serenaded by the humming of atoms trying to catch the light. And then the sensation is gone and the everyday world of effort and ease returns. Yet these glimpses of a kind of transcendent power leave a mark on my being, a knowing that I am capable of much more than I can imagine. The invitation is to use these memories to motivate me to continue to practice. Practice moves possibility toward reality.

The aikido mat is a place of possibility. It is also a testing ground. It is a place where I can test my capacity to manifest the values I believe in and practice in my daily life and my meditation practice – values that include wisdom, compassion, gentleness and strength. We practice by 'attacking' each other so we can learn to more skillfully respond to low-grade threat with wisdom, confidence and compassion.

This capacity to relax, open, and radiate compassion in the face of low-grade threat does not come solely through understanding. It develops through practice – long term, committed practice. This kind of practice will increase your power to work effectively with the challenges in your life. It will help you to become more Noble, Awesome and Shiny.

Noble, Awesome and Shiny Explained

Our Leadership Embodiment tag line is Noble, Awesome and Shiny. It came from an inspired moment many years ago when I was attending an Aikido seminar. My teacher, Mitsugi Saotome Shihan, was teaching a class.

Saotome Sensei's technique has always been beautiful, flowing and powerful. On this day he demonstrated a technique and then gave the signal that we were to practice what he had demonstrated.

We stood up and began to practice, but within a few seconds he stopped us. I could see the frustration in his face as he said, "You are all too stiff; you must relax." Then he again demonstrated the flowing style he wanted us to display.

We began to practice again, and again after a few seconds he stopped us. I could still hear the frustration in his voice as he said, "Now you all look weak and spaced out." Then he closed his eyes, took a breath and said, "I want to see your Noble, I want to see your Awesome, I want to see your Shiny."

I was touched and inspired by these words. I knew what he meant – they represented the essence of the *centered*, powerful, flowing presence he had been displaying. His words spoke to size, warmth, resilience, connection, knowledge and intuition, the aspects of power that allow us to be influential and effective.

Embody Your Noble Dragon

Noble speaks to our posture; it depicts a calm, dignified, courageous way of being. When our dragon is noble it is benevolent and fearless.

> *Inside each of us there is a noble heart. This heart is the source of our finest aspiration for ourselves and the world. It fills us with the courage to act on our aspirations. Our nobility may be obscured at times, covered over with small thoughts or blocked by confused and confusing emotions. But a noble heart lies intact within each of us nonetheless, ready to open and be offered to the world... When we clear away all that blocks it, this heart can change the world.*

> – Karmapa

Cultivate your Awesome Dragon

Awesome is about size, a feeling of expansion. When we cultivate the quality of awesomeness, we radiate out into the world.

The oldest meaning of awesome is something that inspires awe, wonder or excitement. Awesome also implies a sense of great admiration, respect or fear. It generates a feeling of expansiveness, and when someone or something is awesome they are noticed.

Each of us has an awesome, benevolent dragon within us. This awesome dragon quality is able to relate to a vast expansive view of the world. We have a view of life that is huge and magnificent, and we are an intrinsic part of this great expanse.

Connect with Your Shiny Dragon

The whole thing is to learn every day, to get brighter and brighter. That's what this world is about.

– Jay-Z

Shiny implies that we are filled with light. Shiny things are bright and radiate light. When a person is glowing and radiant they are magnetic. Others are attracted to them and will listen to what they have to say.

Like the sun that warms us, our shiny light reflects in other people's hearts and warms their spirit and their soul. The more we shine the more light we bring to the world. As Marianne Williamson wrote, "And as we let our own light shine, we unconsciously give other people permission to do the same. As we are liberated from our own fear, our presence automatically liberates others."

About Leadership Embodiment

Leadership Embodiment is a process derived from the Japanese martial art of Aikido and the tradition of Mindfulness. It is a way to discover how we can act with great wisdom, compassion and courage in the face of life's challenges.

The principles from Aikido are used to meet low-grade threat with courage and creativity. I define low-grade threat as the stressors that trigger us throughout the day: unpleasant email or voicemail, criticism, being ignored, facing delays, and more. Often the most persistent low-grade threat is our own self-critic.

To be clear, I am not referring to life-threatening or traumatic situations. It takes a great deal more time and lots of support to recover from those kinds of stressors. What the Leadership Embodiment process addresses are the everyday irritations and concerns that absorb much of our mental focus and keep us from being relaxed, curious and creative.

The principles from Mindfulness are used to see how much of our life is organized around our concerns and irritations. We learn to recognize our desires and our fears and meet them with courage and compassion. When we accept the unpleasant parts of ourselves, we can relax with the unpleasant parts of other people. Accepting ourselves helps us to nourish our wisdom, compassion and creativity.

The unpleasant parts of ourselves I liken to compost. Composting requires these three components: human management, aerobic conditions and the development of internal biological heat – all of which are present in our mindfulness practice. The process of making compost recycles various organic materials otherwise regarded as waste products – in this case, our negative thoughts and feelings – and produces a "soil conditioner." Mindfulness in the Leadership Embodiment view doesn't attempt to transform our shadow dragon – it includes it as part of the richness of our being.

Our Lives are Organized around Conversations

The underlying theme of Leadership Embodiment as we present it to groups and individuals is to use these tools to have better conversations. Most of our lives are based around conversations and many of our conversations are unskillful. Taming our inner dragons will help us to listen more genuinely, to speak up more clearly and keep difficult conversations going. Sometimes the conversations we have with ourselves are the most difficult and important. That is why we begin with Personal Power; influencing ourselves sets the stage for influencing others.

Understanding Personality and Center

In order to work with ourselves in this process we make a distinction between our reactive and resourceful selves – we call them *Personality* and *Center*.

Personality is defined as the part of ourselves that organizes around trying to create security in our lives. Our *Personality* tries to prevent loss, such as losses of health, property, family, financial stability and status.

Our *Personality* has strategies to manage our anxiety about loss. The Leadership Embodiment model calls these strategies "control," "approval" and "safety." To create the illusion of security, our head uses control, our heart uses approval, and our gut uses safety.

Like the programs that run in the background on our computers, our *Personality* is constantly running concern over potential losses in the background of our daily lives. And like our computers, it takes a certain amount of energy to keep these concerns going. The result is an energy drain on our system, connected to our shadow dragon.

In the Leadership Embodiment model, *Center* is a 'state of being,' not a place in the body. You might have experienced *Center* when you have tapped into what is often called "the zone", "the flow state" or gotten a "second wind." The *centered* state is an experience of being in flow and having energy *come through us*: it is our bigger universal self. When we are in *Center* we experience life as actually coming from outside our skin, through our bodies and into the environment. In the *centered* state we are not separate individuals; we are a part of everything. The *centered* state connects us to our benevolent dragon.

When we shift to the *centered* state our security strategies change from the need to control to gaining a more expansive perception of the situation. Instead of trying to get approval, we experience compassion for ourselves and others. Rather than focusing on being safe, we find the confidence to be awake to what is happening in the present moment.

It's All About the Space

The hallmark of this model and what distinguishes it from other embodiment processes is that we don't focus on the part of us that is inside our skin. We don't try to feel our body or our breath inside of us. We let that be, just as it is. Instead we focus on the space around us. We do this so that we stop experiencing ourselves as a solid individuated 'me'. If we are tight, we let that be – if we are nervous, we let that be. There is no need to make a change. Instead we relate to the part of us that is in the space around us. We reach out into that space and let it support us.

From a scientific point of view nothing is solid, and that includes us. Matter is comprised of atoms, which are vibrating waves of subatomic particles. Yet even though we may understand that we are vibrating energy waves, when we focus inside our body we experience ourselves as if we are solid individual beings. When we extend into the space surrounding us we can more easily relate with the vibrating waves of energy in the space. It is the space around us that gives us access to wisdom, confidence and compassion – our *centered* self.

The LE process offers the opportunity to connect to particular qualities that we invite to come through us so we can access wisdom, compassion and courage. In this book, you'll find details on how to use this process to activate your resourceful self.

Dragons are a Metaphor for Power

Dragons are a metaphor for the wild, limitless part of us – a way of describing the powerful surges that arise through our bodies and trigger behaviors that are often antithetical to what our thoughts are telling us to do. The good thing is that our wild dragons can be trained. Training tames our dragon energy so we can use it to bring wisdom, compassion and courage to our actions.

A dragon is also a symbol; it stands for the potential to live our universal lives – to live our lives fully, beyond cultural constraints that lead to the small life of safety and security. As a symbol a dragon can manifest as malevolent or benevolent action – a shadow dragon or a light dragon. In other words, dragons are a reference for both our destructive behavior and our kind and generous behavior.

Our dragon's benevolent aspects include compassion and inspiration. Its darker aspects can manifest as resentment or greed. As we examine power through the lens of dragon energy, we will see where our strengths and weaknesses lie and discover how to better use our dragon energy to activate benevolent power.

Centering—The Way We Tame Our Dragons

Centering is a series of exercises that change our focus, our gestures and our body's energy patterns – it allows us to see the world from a different vantage point.

Centering is the method we use to tame our dragons. Centering affects the body and the limbic system, a complex group of structures in the brain that is responsible for interpreting emotional responses, storing memories and regulating body functions. The process of centering allows us to manage the intense urges, the dragon energy that arises in the face of the low-grade threats we face in our daily lives.

Centering harnesses the dragon power within us and teaches us to let it flow through us. It enriches our power and our capacity for compassion and confidence. When we think of our life force as a dragon and centering as a way to tame this energy and use it as a force for good, we realize that our life can become exciting and workable. We then begin to enjoy the challenges that we face.

Centering rouses our benevolent dragon and reminds us that we are in this together; it helps us move from the 'me', to the 'we'. Consider the African proverb, "If you want to go fast, go alone. If you want to go far, go together."

Centering Practices Help Us Glimpse a Different Reality

By taking a few seconds to do centering exercises many times a day, you will begin to discover an uplifted, open state, a natural way of being that invites you to becomes who you are: a Noble, Awesome and Shiny person.

The purpose of the centering practice is to shift from being reactive to being resourceful, from being closed to being open, from being separate to being connected. We make that shift by focusing on the space around us and changing the muscle groups we are using. Activating certain muscle groups releases chemicals that change the way our brain functions. When we activate the flexor muscles we use to bend parts of our body, the hormone cortisol is released. An excess of cortisol shuts down the creative, big picture, risk-taking part of our brain. When that happens, we focus on security and survival – our small life.

When we *Center*, we sit up, and extend out, focusing on the space around us. That activates our extensor muscles, releasing the hormone testosterone. Testosterone gives us access to big-picture thinking, creativity and risk taking. Focusing on the space around us gives us a feeling of openness and expansiveness.

Another element of centering is thinking of something that makes us smile. Smiling activates another chemical called oxytocin. It stimulates our caring side and helps to build and maintain social connection. I call oxytocin the 'connector' chemical.

Centering Moments:
Flashes of Enlightenment Throughout the Day

Here is an example of a quick centering practice - take a moment to try it.

 Inhale up and lengthen your spine, exhale down softening your chest. Think of something that makes you smile.

The centering moments can be an opening to glimpse a different reality. An opening is different than an understanding – it involves a shift in our whole being. An opening is a reality-altering experience that changes our perception of how we see the world and our place in it.

While reading this book you will have numerous opportunities to *Center*. I have placed brief centering moments throughout the text so they become part of your experience as you read. These moments of centering take twenty seconds or less, and they will enhance rather than detract from your reading experience.

The idea is to have little moments, little flashes of enlightenment throughout the day. Flashes of enlightenment are instances where desire for praise or fear of blame are suspended, the door to the mystery is opened and the present moment is full of possibility. Surrendering to those moments soothes the dragon driven by need and greed and frees the benevolent dragon to soar into the realms of creativity and innovation.

Over time the flashes accumulate and begin to change the baseline of our behavior. We react less often and for shorter periods of time. We begin to identify with the part of us that lives in the space around us – the light, resilient and resourceful part of ourselves. When we do react, we can *Center* instead of staying in a reactive state. This allows us to see the situation in a different light.

About This Book

The purpose of this book is for you to discover how to grow your capacity to embody all parts of yourself. We are on a lifelong journey with ourselves, and as Trungpa Rinpoche said, "The path is the goal."

In the book, I share the tools that have helped me to tame my dragon, tools that train my body to influence my mind.

The book is organized in four parts.

PART 1 explains why I look at power through the metaphor of a dragon.

PART 2 explains how to work with yourself to develop your personal power.

PART 3 describes social power and influencing others.

PART 4 discusses how to take the learnings and practices forward into your life.

Our dragons are magnificent and beautiful when they are tamed. Enjoy the ride.

PART 1

Setting the Context

Perhaps all the dragons in our lives are princesses who are only waiting to see us act, just once, with beauty and courage.

—Rainer Maria Rilke

CHAPTER 1

Why Dragons?

The bedrock nature of space and time and the unification of cosmos and quantum are surely among science's great 'open frontiers.' These are parts of the intellectual map where we're still groping for the truth - where, in the fashion of ancient cartographers, we must still inscribe 'here be dragons'.

—Martin Rees

Dragons – A Symbol of Power

Power is a dragon and we can learn to ride it, we can choose how we sit astride the movement that is our life. We can sit with dignity, compassion, and humor; or we can sit with resentment and fear, clinging desperately as we try to keep from falling.

"Here be dragons," refers to dangerous or unexplored territories. In medieval times, mapmakers put illustrations of dragons, such as sea monsters and other mythological creatures on uncharted areas where potential dangers were thought to exist. We have uncharted areas within ourselves where potential dangers of fear and anger lurk below the surface while we attempt to find safety and security. It is possible for us to explore these territories and to tame the dragons, turning our fear and anger into wisdom and compassion.

When we think of having a dragon in us, it is a way of seeing ourselves in a different light. It is a way of getting some perspective on ourselves, a way to lighten up and not take things so seriously.

In my meditation room I have a statue of Kuan Yin riding a dragon. Kuan Yin is known in the East as the goddess of mercy and compassion. Because of her compassion she can understand the dragon's nature and stand astride the dragon with grace and ease.

In Tibet, dragons are seen as very positive. The Tibetan dragon is a creature of great creative power: a positive icon, representing the strong male yang principle of heaven, change, energy, wealth and creativity. Dragons are shape shifters, able to transform at will, becoming as small as a silkworm to as large a giant that fills the sky.

In the European chivalric and Christian traditions, however, dragons have been seen to represent the dark side of humanity, including greed, lust, and violence. Recognizing that we have the dark side of dragons within us allows us to address our propensity for security and greed.

We Can Tame Our Wild Dragons

If we really want to be effective in the world we need to spend less time fighting and struggling with ourselves and wanting others to be different. Acknowledging the dark part of ourselves and making friends with our darker dragon is the first step to taming it.

My training in martial arts has taught me that I have the ability to tame my own wild dragons: my aggression and my greed. I have learned that when I am tense, I struggle more with execution of the martial arts techniques and I become more fatigued and less creative. I find myself trying to suppress my irritation or rationalize that I have a right to be irritated. This is the dark side of my humanity. It is my compost, my fertilizer, and when I use it properly it blossoms into insight, wisdom and compassion. Learning to tame this dark side allows me moments when my two dragons become one, seething with humanity and the potential for power and love.

Dragons as Protectors

...I would not want to live in a world without dragons, as I would not want to live in a world without magic, for that is a world without mystery, and that is a world without faith.

–R. A. Salvatore

In some wisdom traditions dragons are considered protectors. They protect the integrity of wisdom and compassion. They contain the surges and impulses that course through us and awaken our basic goodness. When we connect to our benevolent dragon, we are reminded that we are not alone – that there is a universal urge toward light and the evolution of life.

But in order for our dragons to become protectors they need training. We need a process to keep our dragon energy from running wild and becoming destructive. We need a process to cultivate a dragon that is Noble, Awesome and Shiny.

 Inhale and lengthen your spine, take a long exhale toward the earth, open your arms for three seconds

Dragons Represent our Nature

I read books about dragons to my children and then to my grandchildren. We would read them over and over.

In those books, dragons sometimes represented positive aspects of nature – mountains, rivers, clouds, rainbows, thunder and lightning. Sometimes they represented the darker aspects of human nature like greed. There are stories of dragons that hoard gold, abduct fair maidens and feed on children. Then there are the stories of protector dragons that subdue earthquakes and raging torrents, and others about dragons that protect maidens and become rainbows showering gold and granting wishes to poor villagers.

In those stories, for a dragon to show up, there would be a need for some kind of intervention. Someone would have to be worthy to call upon a dragon and brave enough to face such a powerful force.

So how do we find the part of ourselves that is worthy and brave? I believe these qualities arise from practice, from training, from something beyond pure mental understanding.

Summoning Your Dragon Takes Practice

In Leadership Embodiment practices we summon our power; we call upon our dragon to emerge from the depths of our spirit. We do this to enliven and empower our conversations with ourselves and with others.

There is a particular process for managing the energy of power. When the power arises, it is contained and organized in a circle or triangle shape.

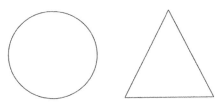

Because this practice comes from martial arts, and not psychology, we are not as interested in understanding power as we are in using it skillfully. If you watch sports you may understand the play or how the movement should go, but that doesn't mean you could execute the play or the movement.

To actually be able to skillfully use power when you are facing a state of low-grade threat, you need to practice. In this view practices are exercises or 'drills', as they say in sports. The drills allow a person in sports to play their game with greater creativity and flexibility. The centering practices suggested in this book are designed to help people play the 'game of life' with more creativity and confidence and compassion.

In the Leadership Embodiment model we use different ways to summon our power. We push on each other physically; we use Japanese style wooden swords called bokken. We use the swords because when you put a stick, especially one shaped like a sword, in a human's hands a great deal of energy surges through the body. We organize that energy by teaching the body how to make a straight cut in the air. This practice gives form and clarity to the energy surging through the body.

We also make a verbal declaration of our intention to manifest something in the world. We make the cut with our bokken or use our hands to make a triangle while saying out loud what we want to accomplish. I might say something like, "I want to give people tools to be more compassionate leaders." With repeated practice, we learn how to organize, focus and relax as the energy surges through our bodies. We become more comfortable and familiar with the surges of power that arise in moments of excitement. Our personal space expands in order to manage the sword so we develop the capacity to expand our energy even when we are not holding the sword.

Repeating the verbal declaration brings clarity and focus to what we want to accomplish. This is a great tool to prepare for important conversations because a person with clarity and a large presence gets more of a voice. This doesn't mean that others will always agree but it does mean that people will listen.

These body practices begin to train the dragon, allowing us to organize the intense energy and power within us. These practices allow us to align with our positive intention and activate our benevolent dragon.

We impact the environment with the quality and intensity of the energy that emanates from us. When our energy is strong and expansive it affects everything around us. Size matters, but it is not the size of our bicep, but the size of our spirit that counts. In this view, size does not refer to physical dimensions. There is a *YouTube* video of a mongoose intimidating three lionesses in which the mongoose, though much smaller physically, has a much bigger presence energetically.

Your body may not be big physically, but you can be sure that your inner dragons have big energy. As The Dalai Lama pointed out, "If you think you are too small to make a difference, try sleeping with a mosquito."

Why is it so Hard to Tame our Dragons?

Most people I have met want to lead happy, healthy, generous lives. Many of them have read books or taken courses on self-development or meditation and mindfulness. They know how they would like to be in the world. They want work-life balance, to be comfortable materially and to be able to be calm and generous in the face of unpleasant circumstances. They want to like themselves and have fun rather than to worry and constantly judge themselves and others. Yet most people spend more time worrying and criticizing themselves and others than they do enjoying and appreciating their lives. Why is this so?

It is not that people don't understand the importance of leading happy, healthy lives. They do understand; yet they cannot live the kind of lives they know would make them happy and healthy. They cannot live with ease because they are in the habit of being critical, concerned and irritated. And habits are hard to break because that would mean they would have to change.

Our ego, or our *personality*, is afraid of change. Our *personality* references on security and this part of us has a story about why we are the way we are and why we need to keep it that way – the urge for homeostasis. We are afraid that if we let down our guard, if we imagine that our lives are more than what our education and culture taught us to believe, then some demon dragon will rise from within and terrorize our lives. And so we hold on tight to our small selves; hoping that if we don't rock the boat, it won't capsize.

 Inhale and uplift your posture, take a few seconds to focus on the space around you.

CHAPTER 2

About Power

Come not between the dragon and his wrath.

—William Shakespeare, *King Lear*

What is it about Power that Frightens Us?

Let's take a deeper look into this notion of power. What are we afraid of?

We are afraid of failure, criticism and exhaustion; we are afraid that, as Lord Acton famously wrote, "Absolute power corrupts absolutely." And we are right; these are real and possible outcomes. We intuitively know that power will put us in the spotlight and we will receive scrutiny for every action we take. We may lose our privacy and people will project their fears and desires on us.

We recognize that power can make us greedy and self-centered. There is a survival tendency to act from a perspective of scarcity, triggering the urge to hunker down and stay safe. When we try to create security for ourselves at the expense of others we are not going to be Noble, Awesome and Shiny. We will not be able to access our benevolent power.

It takes effort, understanding, courage and compassion to learn to manage our power skillfully. So why should we make the effort? I believe the urge to cultivate benevolent power is an evolutionary urge to become a greater vessel for wisdom, compassion and creativity. Our fear of loss can keep us alert to the trap of self-serving behavior.

How do we make the choice of which dragon will serve us? Our fears are valid. Issues of power can lead to conflict: conflict with others as well as inner conflict. We can feel pulled in two directions – we want to protect ourselves and we care about others. The question is – can our desire to be of service become stronger than our fear of scrutiny and scarcity?

Yet if you have glimpsed what it is like to be part of something bigger, to be moved by a flow so strong that you only have to relax and enjoy high performance, you already have the seed of universal energy in your awareness. Your soul will not rest in a limited half-life – you want more, you sense that, as Marianne Williamson wrote, "Our deepest fear is not that we are inadequate. Our deepest fear is that we are powerful beyond measure. It is our light, not our darkness that most frightens us." Some people have been told that they are 'too much, too powerful'. My experience is that when power is tempered by warmth, it is never 'too much'.

The Dynamics of Power

Power is a system of interactions that is driven by the evolution of life. As we grow and evolve, power dynamics change around us and within us. Power is not simplistic, and people can share power equally for only a short period of time. If you have 'power with' for a moment, at some point there will be a question as to who has more power.

Power is dynamic and given that people are innately competitive there will always be power dynamics and continuous adjustments in the relationships around power. From dictators to slaves, how we interact to support and to dominate situations has to do with how we are perceived and how we perceive ourselves.

From an early age we experience who has power and how they use it. As children we experience the ways our caretakers use power to control us, other people, and their environment. At some point we become aware that we have the power to affect the people around us. We begin to explore how that power works and experience the positive and negative consequences of our actions.

As our ego develops and we begin to have a sense of a separate self, we begin to organize around ways of creating security. We look for ways to be connected, to avoid rejection, so we are not outside the group. The animal part of us does not want to be isolated – safety lies in the group, the community, the tribe.

Tribes and communities are never flat. From the time we began on the savanna, right through to the evolution of Maslow's hierarchies of needs, humans organize them selves around power and power has many faces. There are those who feel they are powerful, those who align with those they perceive as powerful, those who resist those they perceive as powerful and those who ignore those they perceive as powerful.

As the cliché says, "it is not a matter of *if*, it is a matter of *when...*" we use power and it is used on us. What we can do is recognize the effects of how we use power and how power is being used on us. This recognition can awaken us to the realization that we have choice – we can choose how we use power and how we use it with others. We can choose to engage in practices that help us learn to relax when we feel energy and power coursing through us.

How Myths Shed Light on our Fears

Dragons are mythical, and what is a myth if not a way of explaining natural or social phenomena? Reality is relative;

some things that people in one culture believe are considered a myth in a different culture.

For example, in China, mothers are not supposed to bathe, to go outside, have a shower or drink cold water for an entire month following childbirth. The women are advised to stay indoors for recovery from the trauma of birth and feed the newborn baby. Yet in the United States childbirth is not considered to be a trauma and mothers bathe their infants and take them outside within the first few days.

Seeing a cultural behavior as a myth is a way of going beyond the limitations that the culture has placed on our actions. We can choose not to be limited by our cultural beliefs. Instead, we can find creative ways to move beyond what we were taught. In the seventies, counter culture mothers in California were viewing the mandate that one must give birth in a hospital with drugs was a myth that was no longer valid. They started having babies at home with midwives and family in attendance. They created a culture that was no longer afraid of natural childbirth.

When we realize that cultural beliefs, like the idea that a woman must give birth in a hospital, are not founded in truths but in habits of behaviors, we can consider them to be myths. We can see that they are founded in fear and understand that we can choose how we act in those situations. Cultural fears are only one aspect of how we engage with fear, we also experience internal fears that we cannot explain or understand.

Our inner experience can be wild, destructive and greedy. Myths can help us look at the dark parts of ourselves through another lens. Whether we choose to experience these attributes as demon dragons is up to each of us, but psychology and mythology both point to the fact that we have feelings that seem out of control. Call them moods, emotions, or archetypes –

they exist. We need to find skillful ways of managing and
training these urges. Doing that takes the practice of Centering.

 *Inhale and uplift, exhale and soften thinking of something
that makes you smile, straighten your arms for 3 seconds.*

Centering is a Way to Tame Our Dragons

Centering allows us to connect with our bigger expansive self
and cultivate positive attributes – size, warmth, resilience,
connection, knowledge and intuition. Centering helps to tame
our dragon, cultivate our 'basic goodness', and become a little
more Noble, Awesome and Shiny.

Let's revisit the distinctions between *Personality* and *Center*.
Remember our *Personality* is defined as the part of us that
organizes around trying to create security in our lives. This part
of us identifies as an individual that is separate from other
individuals.

By closing our eyes and going inside to feel the breath or energy
running through us, we identify with an individual sense of
'me'. We say things like, "My body is tight, my breath is short or
I breathe down into my belly." Experiencing ourselves as
separate individuals we find ways to manage our interactions
with others; we connect with them, argue with them, play with
them and so on.

Center is a different part of our selves, it is a 'state of being' not
a place in the body. Our *Centered* Self is our bigger universal
Self, it is the part of us that exists outside our skin. This part of
us knows that we are not a separate individual self, it knows we
are naturally interconnected with all things. This bigger Self,
our *Centered* Self, has the awareness that we are made of atoms

– vibrating energy that allows wisdom, compassion and courage to flow through us.

Centering shifts our state of being from our separate individuated self to our expansive interconnected Self. When *centered*, we change the muscle groups we are using; the different muscle groups change our hormones, which changes the way our brain functions. This shift changes the stories we tell ourselves. The view that I am a negative, problematic person because I am so judgmental is replaced. By sitting up and extending out to see the big picture, I see myself as a person whose negative tendencies are trying to keep me safe.

As Neil Degrasse Tyson said –

> *The atoms of our bodies are traceable to stars that manufactured them in their cores and exploded these enriched ingredients across our galaxy, billions of years ago. For this reason, we are biologically connected to every other living thing in the world. We are chemically connected to all molecules on Earth. And we are atomically connected to all atoms in the universe. We are not figuratively, but literally stardust.*

CHAPTER 3

The Power of Centering

Love is the bond between people, the way to teach and the center of the world.

—Jose Marti

Our Strategies for Creating Security

When we are operating from *Center* we are in the flow and we can relax, see possibilities and act without fear. It would be wonderful if we could live from this place consistently, but sadly this is not the case. No one stays *centered*.

When we experience stress that is triggered by low-grade threat our *Personality* takes over. Our darker dragon surfaces and we become tense and defensive. We begin to use the strategies we have created as a defense mechanism.

One strategy might be to convince ourselves that if we keep everything under control we will be safe. Another is to get the approval — but just the right amount so we won't feel anxious because oddly, too much approval can make us uncomfortable and insecure. It takes a lot of energy to get the right amount of approval, so this strategy can be very tiring.

Still another strategy we use to create the illusion of security is called "safety." The goal of this approach is to be sure that actions are done the correct way even if it means that things get out of control or people disapprove of you. If you are a person who uses this strategy, you will employ it regardless of the consequences.

These strategies and their variations take a lot of energy to maintain. Often we are so used to these behaviors we don't realize that they are strategies – we believe that this is how we make our way in the world.

Recognizing the ways in which we try to create security for ourselves can help us see how deeply ingrained these behaviors are. They will probably always be part of our response to whatever we perceive as a low-grade threat. If we are willing to accept these patterns as our starting place, then we don't have to try to transform ourselves. We can use centering to trigger an alternative pattern that allows us to engage with the low-grade threat in a different way.

Our reactive patterns can become an opportunity to *Center* and activate our benevolent dragon. Instead of organizing around security we can train ourselves to use the centering process to organize around what might be possible. We can relate to our bigger resourceful self – the self that lies outside our skin. We can discover that we are not just a limited, separate self; we are powerful, creative, vibrant, compassionate and connected to all things.

Discomfort is a Natural Part of Life

In the west, and in many of the advanced countries, we are obsessed with comfort. We believe that material things – bigger houses, fancy cars and designer clothes will make us feel comfortable. We are concerned that we will be uncomfortable and attempt to protect ourselves from possible discomfort.

We worry that we will feel cramped, cold or hot, full or empty, tired, or anxious. We are concerned about being criticized or disrespected. It is difficult to experience our power when we are struggling with and resisting discomfort. In fact when we resist discomfort we often feel powerless.

What we need to remember is that all of the above is going to occur. When we shift to our *centered* more expansive self we can relax with discomfort. Rather than worrying about how uncomfortable we are, we could say to ourselves, "Oh look, now is the time when I am tired, now is the time when I am cramped."

We could learn to accept that discomfort is a natural part of life. Like the sun going down and coming up, times of comfort and discomfort are inevitable. Our experience keeps changing and if we know how to *Center* ourselves we can adapt to the changes with more grace and ease. We can more easily summon our benevolent dragon.

 Uplift your posture; focus on the space and think of something that makes you smile.

Centering is the Key to Recovery

In the Introduction, I explained what Centering is and how it connects with Dragons. Let's unpack it a bit more. The more we understand, the better we are at recovering our *centered* state.

When we first start working with ourselves, our personalities tend to be agitated or dull. Our personality has not been tamed; it is a wild dragon, in the habit of wanting comfort, approval and material things. We read books and listen to talks about how to be kind and creative. We are told that if we are generous, compassionate and inspiring, we will be happy and satisfied. Yet when we try to implement these practices, we lose focus and end up wanting comfort, control and appreciation.

We have been 'thrown off' our resolution and return to agitation or dullness.

The centering process is easy to do. Remember when we change the muscle groups we are using, just by sitting up and straightening our arms; the different muscle groups change the hormones which changes the way the brain functions. It is a short cut to change the muscle groups in the body. It is worth repeating that changing the body changes the brain. When our muscles are tight our brain is tight.

The key to taming the dragon is to get back to our *centered* state. When we are *centered*, we are not focused inside our body. Instead, we are focused on the space around our body – on the part of us that connects us to all things. The *centered* state is not driven by our security needs; it is oriented to the vibrating life force that surrounds us.

Based on my experience in martial arts I discovered that centering can be quick and simple. If your stress levels are not too high you will be able to recover your *centered* state in less than twenty seconds. When you *Center* you are in a more relaxed state, your body can find more balance and you will be increasing your health and wellbeing.

Try it:

 Inhale up and lengthen your spine, exhale down and think of something that makes you smile.

That is it!

You can *Center* in as little as five seconds.

 Uplift your posture, expand out and settle.

If you have a little more time:

 Inhale up toward the sky lengthening your spine, then exhale down toward the earth thinking of something that makes you smile. Expand out in all directions and focus on the space around you.

Here's another one:

 Breathe in your irritation or concerns for two or three seconds – then exhale appreciation or generosity for six seconds. Repeat two or three times.

Often when I am walking I simply use this mantra – *'long neck, long fingers, light and open.'*
There is a one-second practice for those of you who 'have no time'. Have you ever seen a lizard doing what is called 'lizard push-ups'? They extend their legs and then crouch down over and over. You can see them doing it to music on *YouTube*. It can take just one second to *sit up straighter and extend out*, and then you can let it go.

 Do a lizard pushup, sit up straighter and extend out.

If you apply these centering practices throughout the day you will maintain a greater sense of balance and wellbeing. You will be able to access more insight, humor and compassion. You will still find yourself reacting to irritations and concerns. When that happens, you can acknowledge, "Oh yes, I am reacting again." You don't have to stay in that reactive state. In fact, your reactivity can become a doorway to a centering practice.

To recover your *Center*, you now have a set of practices that will take only one to twenty seconds each. And if you haven't got one second – well, you are in serious trouble.

Think of a Double Helix

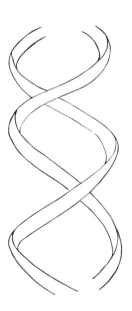

Centering is easier to do when it is interesting and engaging. One way to enhance the focus on breath is to think of it as a double helix like a DNA strand. I love that image. It feels cosmic and organic at the same time.

Here's how I use it: When I inhale, I follow the spiral up through my body and imagine it continues right through the top of my head. On the exhale, I follow the spiral from above my head down through my body toward the earth.

To enhance the focus even more I think of my breath as a thermal. Thermals are updrafts of warm air that rise from the ground into the sky. By flying in a spiraling circular path within these columns of rising air, birds are able to "ride" the air currents and climb to higher altitudes while expending very little energy in the process. Where I live I can watch birds ride the thermals without flapping their wings. They soar up on the spiral at the center of the thermal; they float down on the spiral that is the outside of the thermal. Like the birds I can ride the thermal of my breath – soaring up on the inhale and floating down on the exhale.

Try it for a few breaths. Inhale spiraling up toward the sky and exhale floating down toward the earth.

Another way to think about the energy pattern of our body and breath is to visualize a fountain. In the very core along your spine the movement bubbles up toward the sky. Around the outside of your body the movement is flowing down.

This visualization can activate a feeling of lightness along the vertical center of your being and a softness on the outside, softening behind the eyes, the jaw, shoulders, chest and belly.

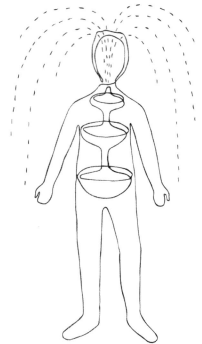

Visualize a fountain inside your body.

 Try it for a few breaths: on the inhale, the fountain bubbles up. On the exhale, flow down and let your muscles soften and relax.

Changing the Story — The Alchemy of an Alternative World View

To live up to our full potential and tap into our power, we need different stories about who we are. We are not just our *personality*. We also have a powerful, vibrant, expansive, universal self, a benevolent dragon. Let's work on that story –

who are the heroes and heroines? What are the challenges? What is the landscape? How does this story unfold?

This process is not so much about transformation as it is about inclusion. We are both our *personality* and our *centered* selves. Our dragons have a self-serving shadow side and a wise benevolent side. In order to have more access to our benevolent power and potential, we need to shift the baseline from spending most of our time in our limited *personality* to spending more of our time in our *centered*, universal, benevolent dragon self.

When we *center* we change our state, which changes the story, which changes our behavior. We can connect to heroes and heroines instead of focusing on villains and anti-heroes.

Training Tames our Dragon

No one plays a sport or goes to a gym or a martial arts mat to be 'relaxed and comfortable'. They go to train so they can become stronger and more proficient – so they can feel more powerful and more effective. No one takes on the process of earning a PhD so they can feel relaxed and comfortable during that process. They take on the rigors so they can become competent, an expert in that field – they do it so they can feel more powerful. We are not born with expertise; we develop it through study, practice and discipline.

> The mind is like an elephant, a well trained elephant is very useful and a poorly trained elephant is very dangerous.
>
> —Tibetan saying.

Whether we use the metaphor of a dragon, a horse or an elephant, we are pointing to the same thing – the idea that we all have power; we have something big and strong inside of us, a deep drive to manifest security in our lives. That power shows up as ego or *personality* and left unchecked can wreak havoc on our body and mind. Every culture seeks to find a way to manage and contain this drive. For generations we have sought ways to tame the wildness.

I find the idea of being able to ride this energy with skill very appealing. When I was young I heard a saying like, "You must take the reins of life and guide it where you want to go." Later, when I became a hippie, the rhetoric was more like, "Stay in the saddle and see where it takes you; go along for the ride."

In both cases the metaphor was that life is a ride. For me this is an especially apt metaphor because I grew up riding horses. Now the life I ride is more like a dragon than a horse. Dragons are powerful, beautiful, scary and magnificent. I want to be able to ride the dragon of my life with elegance and grace. And I want the wisdom to know when to take the reins and guide the dragon, and when simply to go along for the ride. I want to be able to keep my seat with strength and gentleness, and when I fall off I want to be able to get right back on, recover my seat and continue with a mind of curiosity and an open heart.

My experience is that my time working with horses allowed me to excel in aikido. The principles and practices are the same. The experience of working with a big, strong power and finding a way to manage that power with beauty and flow is what connects both disciplines. As an aikido teacher I have noticed that people who have trained horses also excel when they come to train aikido.

When we train with power, we discover that we need more than understanding. We need to train our body to train our mind. I have learned from aikido training that my body reacts before my mind realizes what is going on. Since my body leads my mind, it is the body that needs to train to develop skillful patterns and practices that help me to stay open and resourceful in unpleasant circumstances. My mind is my starting point; it has to want to ride the dragon with elegance and grace. But it is my body that actually allows me to do it in difficult moments, in the face of low-grade threats.

When I come to the aikido mat, I begin by bowing before I step onto the mat. The bow can represent many things. But from a pragmatic perspective it gives me a moment to recognize that I am going to put myself in a training situation. I will be dealing with attacks and learning to throw and fall. To learn, I need to be awake and alert. I suggest the same approach when you prepare to ride the dragon of life.

When learning to ride a horse, the first thing you do is to connect with the horse. You let the horse see you and smell you, you pat the horse to communicate friendliness. Brute force is not the best way to direct a huge animal like a horse. So it is with life. Trying to be in control and make everything happen the way you want will not give you a sense of flow and grace. Being calm, kind and respectful will give you a much more enjoyable ride.

 Inhale and lighten up, exhale and soften, open up a little more.

The Value of a Ritual

We have established that to begin the day it is best to be alert and friendly toward whatever may come your way. The easiest way to do this is to have a ritual.

A ritual is a ceremony consisting of a series of actions performed according to a prescribed order — anything from taking a few seconds to *Center*, to a morning run, a good workout, meditation or yoga practice. To progress at dragon riding you will need to do the activity you choose every day – or at least five days a week. You need to do it no matter how you feel.

Your ritual will help you discipline yourself so you can take control of your life, so that you can guide the dragon where you want to go. You can think of your morning ritual as getting on the dragon.

For many people having support is key to keeping the discipline of a ritual. Having a friend, a teacher or a community that also cultivates ways to discover positive power can give us a 'leg up.' Going to yoga classes or weekly meditation meetings provides a sense that there are other people who are also engaged in rituals. This can help sustain your commitment and create momentum for long-term committed practice.

Support can manifest in many ways. For some, places in nature or being with animals reconnects the spirit to a sense of power, wholeness and benevolence. Nowadays people have communities online or listen to podcasts. I suggest using anything and everything that will support training your dragon to show up as Noble, Awesome and Shiny.

PART 2

Influencing Ourselves

The most powerful moral influence is example.

— Huston Smith

CHAPTER 4

Personal Power—

Summoning Your Benevolent Dragon

When we *Center* we have the ability to influence ourselves - to generate wisdom, confidence and compassion.

 Take a few seconds to uplift, expand and relax.

How do we train our inner dragon so we can open our hearts and let our light shine? We need to develop our personal power.

I break personal power into six aspects or characteristics, each of which is a component for developing our capacity to live in a way we choose, a way that makes us feel comfortable with ourselves, happy to keep our own company, and effective in our actions. The aspects are Motivation, Inspiration, Discipline, Big Picture, Compassion and Confidence.

These aspects of personal power invite us to develop the strength to follow our hearts even when others do not support us. The dark side of our inner dragons wants the impossible – security and immortality. If we don't pay attention, we will sell our soul to that which distracts us from the necessary work of summoning our benevolent dragon.

Examining the characteristics of our personal power helps us understand which areas need more attention so we know where to apply our centering practice. Our centering allows us to train our inner dragon so we can deepen our capacity to manifest the aspects of personal power in our daily life.

The six aspects are, for all practical purposes, a circle or parts of a whole.

For me they unfold in the order below, starting with Motivation. For you, the entry point may be somewhere else on the circle

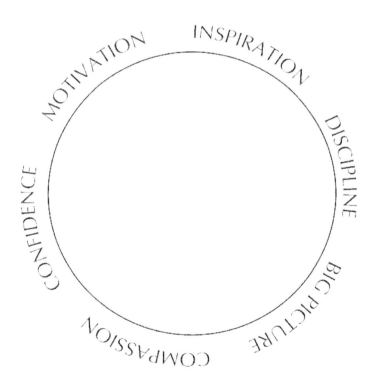

Motivation

You're braver than you believe, stronger than you seem and smarter than you think.

—Christopher Robin

Motivation is defined as, "The reason or reasons one has for acting or behaving in a particular way." How do we find the reasons that activate our desire to contribute – to serve others? When I have asked this question in my workshops, participants have suggested words like "vision," "potential," and "purpose." To find your Motivation, look for a word that best represents this particular aspect of personal power for you.

Why Do We Act?

Let's take a moment to consider why we act. Our reasons could range from basic survival to altruistic urges to serve for the greater good. For each of us there is a certain percentage of actions intended to secure our physical and emotional comfort. For example, we might get up and go to work because there is security in that activity. The need to act for security might be driven by financial stability or it might be motivated by the need for image stability – we might want people to think we are good or successful or diligent or brave. If we didn't go to work, we might feel bored or unimportant.

Is there something beyond security that energizes us to get up and go to work? Perhaps we have an urge to do something that will be helpful in the world. I believe that in each of us there is a benevolent dragon that as Rainer Maria Rilke wrote, 'is wanting to act with beauty and courage'. We all have what Trungpa Rinpoche called 'basic goodness', a capacity that is alive and well within each of us. This basic goodness is the benevolent urge to serve, to be helpful and strong on behalf of others.

In each of us lies a protector dragon. This doesn't mean that we aren't afraid – courage is defined as, "The ability to do something that frightens one." Most of the great, compassionate and powerful leaders in history were afraid and angry. Georgia O'Keeffe, the American painter said, "I've been absolutely terrified every moment of my life - and I've never let it keep me from doing a single thing I wanted to do."

It is important to acknowledge the dragons that show up as fear and anger. The art is to know how much time to spend acknowledging those emotions. If we spend too long, we will indulge in the negative emotions; if we don't give enough time and attention, we will be pushing them away. We can lose our Motivation and become distracted by fear and anger if we are not skillful with ourselves.

When we are skillful we can summon the benevolent dragon within us to show up and lead us through our day. Learning to tame our dragon helps us to keep our Motivation strong.

The Shadow Side of Motivation

Motivational speakers often emphasize the more self-serving aspect of Motivation. They focus on helping the individual "me" achieve personal happiness and success and financial abundance, not on serving others or supporting a cause. This kind of Motivation speaks to the security part of our nature, the part of us that wants to have and to hold – not release and open.

Spiritual teachers, on the other hand, generally encourage the importance of connecting to something bigger than the individual self. For instance in Tibetan Buddhism there is a practice called taking *The Bodhisattva vow,* which is the vow taken by Mahayana Buddhists to liberate all sentient beings. It is a vow they take to devote themselves to the service of others. Helping others is one of the core principles of Islam. The South African noun *Ubuntu* is often translated as "I am because we are," or "humanity towards others", and can be used in a more philosophical sense to mean the belief in a universal bond of sharing that connects all humanity.

This sentiment, that serving others is key to living a good and benevolent life, can be found over and over throughout the world. As the inspirational Buddhist teacher Thich Nhat Hanh wrote, "When you look deeply, you see the pain and suffering in the world, and recognize your deep desire to relieve it. You also recognize that bringing joy to others is the greatest joy you can have, the greatest achievement. In choosing to cultivate true power, you do not have to give up your desire for the good life. Your life can be more satisfying, and you will be happy and relaxed, relieving suffering and bringing happiness to everyone."

Waking the Benevolent Dragon

Thus, the point of tapping the Motivation to serve is to awaken our benevolent impulses—our benevolent dragon. Waking this benevolent dragon begins to shift the baseline of our actions from serving ourselves to serving others. Of course we will continue to be motivated by our security needs as well, but we will be able to spend more time in our service mode and less in our security mode.

 Uplift, expand and settle. Inhale lengthening your spine, exhale softening your chest, think of something that makes you smile.

Take a moment to ask yourself – how many of your actions are based on self-preservation? How many are based on serving others? Is that how you want to live your life? Is that how you want to use your power?

The cool thing about being human is that we have the power to affect our actions. Programs like Alcoholics Anonymous have shown that we can actually change the way we live in the world. This is both the invitation and the challenge: to activate our benevolent dragon more often, to choose to cultivate service-oriented practices. The question is.... How? One way is to call upon Inspiration. And a classic way to do that is to use archetypes.

Inspiration

The things you do for yourself are gone when you are gone, but the things you do for others remain as your legacy.

—Kalu Ndukwe Kalu

Inspiration is an experience of possibility — it arouses our heart; it stimulates our interest and creativity. But Inspiration is often clouded by concerns and irritations, usually triggered by security needs.

These concerns and irritations make us react negatively to situations that are not going the way we want them to go. It is important to recognize when we are becoming reactive and it is important to be kind to our unskillful reactive self. We need to remember that whatever arises in our mind and heart is valid. It is an attempt at creating security.

For example, I am frequently judgmental and, if I am not attentive, I will criticize myself for that behavior. When I am attentive I can remind myself that it is a habit from my childhood when being judgmental made me feel that I was right, and if I was right, I felt safe. So now I can say to myself, "Ah, you are trying to keep me safe." I can be tender and kind for a few seconds, and then I can *Center* and shift to my more compassionate and inspirational self, my *centered* self.

This shift changes the story. Instead of seeing myself as a negative, problematic person because I am so judgmental, when I sit up and extend out I see the Big Picture. I see myself as a person with some negative tendencies that are only trying to keep me safe.

 Inhale lengthen the spine, exhale softening the chest, notice the space in the room.

In this way, I sooth the dragon of judgment so that it doesn't destroy Inspiration. When I am *centered*, I feel more inspired and can see myself as someone capable of wise, compassionate action.

In our Leadership Embodiment work, we give participants 'posse cards' with photos of famous inspirational people, scenes of nature and positive quotes. We ask them to choose a few cards that resonate for them. If we are presenting at a conference, we might bring four to six hundred cards. They are often gone on the first day.

That people love these cards speaks to how much they long for Inspiration and their deep desire to awaken the connection to heroes and heroines. These heroes and heroines do not have to be famous; they can be a friend, a family member or a pet. Think of the feeling you get when you look at a photo of a loved one. Perhaps you smile involuntarily or get a warm feeling in your heart. Perhaps there is a feeling of longing for connection. You can remind yourself that you are not separate; you are connected.

Think about who or what you can put in your posse. Who or what will inspire you and connect you with wisdom, Compassion and courage? For instance one of the practices I use to trigger Compassion is to think of Mother Teresa while inviting her quality of Compassion to come through me. As I open myself to the Compassion of Mother Teresa for a few seconds or even a moment, I am touched by more warmth, kindness and care for the world.

This feeling of Compassion is always available and yet it is difficult to access when I look inside myself. When I go inside to find Compassion, I also find guilt and shame; so the level of Compassion is not as strong and clear as it is when I focus outside my skin. It is quicker and easier to access Inspiration when I think of it as surrounding me and flowing through me.

When I invite Compassion to come through me, it is still me –a more clean and clear version of me. My Inspirational dragon can spread its wings and soar, free to imagine possibilities.

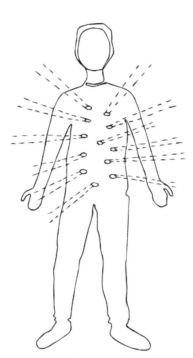

Inspiration flowing through you

 Inspiration flowing through you
Uplift, expand and settle

The Shadow Side of Inspiration

Like all aspects of human behavior, Inspiration has a shadow side. It might emerge as a drive to have more riches or influence over others. Following this kind of Inspiration leads to a dark power. The dark dragon that always wants more. This dragon is not content and compassionate; it is in a state of continuous want.

In Tibetan Buddhism there are realms of suffering similar to Dante's levels of hell in his book, *The Inferno*. The realm of continuous wanting is called the realm of the 'hungry ghosts'. The beings there are depicted as having large mouths and large stomachs and very small throats. They want more but their small throat does not allow them to take in what their large stomachs are hungering for. They are always hungry and can never be satisfied.

So how do we keep focused on the positive aspect of Inspiration? How do we stay connected to our altruistic, benevolent ways of being? I suggest that Discipline is the key to cultivating positive actions.

Many years ago I was inspired by Parmahansa Yoganada's wonderful book *Autobiography of a Yogi* to begin a meditation practice. Anyone who has ever started meditating knows how important it is to have Discipline. Parmahansa Yoganada's statement regarding willpower points to how important this capacity is for developing personal power. He said, "Willpower is like a light switch that must be turned on before electricity can flow to the bulb. Dynamic and persistent willpower is one of the most powerful forces in the universe." That statement makes it clear that another aspect of the personal power process is Discipline.

Discipline

To tame ourselves is the only way we can change and improve the world.

—Lama Yeshe Losal Rinpoche

Our dragon needs Discipline, not a heavy handed Discipline but a gentle, firm Discipline. Discipline allows our dragon to organize its energy so we can make choices.

There are many ways we can apply Discipline. We can establish positive habits of self-care around what we eat, how much we sleep, what exercise we take, and what we watch online. When we Discipline ourselves around these areas we develop positive habits that allow us to live more healthy lives and have more energy.

Discipline allows us to create habits that can activate our brain's positive thought pathways. Without Discipline we can fall into unhealthy behaviors and negative habits of acting and thinking. One of my favorite quotes from the Buddha highlights this principle, "As irrigators lead water where they want, as archers make their arrows straight, as carpenters carve wood, so the wise shape their minds."

 Lighten up, extend your arms think of something that makes you smile.

Mindfulness: Making Friends With Ourselves

Mindfulness helps us stay accountable to our aspirations and intentions, make friends with ourselves and awaken the basic goodness that is the essence of our spiritual life.

In the Leadership Embodiment model we view mindfulness as an opportunity to sit down with yourself and observe your thoughts. Thoughts tend to arise in repetitive patterns. Once the thought patterns are noticed, it is easier to see them as habits rather than believing them as being right or true.

The time you spend meditating is also a way of relating with yourself. You can begin to make friends with your personality and all the different aspects of your mind. You can begin tolerating and accepting the positive and negative parts of yourself.

We sit down and clarify our posture – hips are higher than the knees so the pelvis is stable and tipped slightly forward bringing weight into the knees or feet. Our eyes are open and our hands are resting on the thighs.

As we inhale we uplift our posture, lengthening the back of the neck and out the top of the head. The exhale flows down toward the earth in the front of the body softening the chest and belly. We focus at least three breaths in this way to encourage a strong, uplifted feeling in the back and a soft, settled feeling in the front. We use a three-part concentration to stabilize our attention. First we focus on our posture, next we relate with the space around us, and then we follow our breath.

In this view we find that it is helpful to categorize types of thought such as: judging, planning and desiring. Categorizing thoughts lets us see that we have habits of repetitive thinking. Once we realize that we think in habits we can make a choice to think differently and begin changing the habit. For instance, if I recognize that I am judging, I can choose to be curious rather than thinking that I am right.

We work with two basic elements of attention – *awareness* and concentration. *Awareness* is the practice of seeing and being with what is arising in the moment – we are curious about what kind of thoughts are arising. *Concentration* is the practice of focusing one's attention in a particular way so that our energy stabilizes in a contained process of attention. In most styles of meditation focusing on the breath is the most common concentration; some approaches use a mantra, repetition of words, or visualizations.

The Art of Working With Yourself

The art of working with yourself is to find the rhythm in shifting between concentration and awareness. The invitation is not to indulge your thoughts and not to push the thoughts away with concentration. The exercise is to be disciplined about how long to be with and acknowledge the thoughts and feelings before releasing them into the space and returning to the uplifted posture and breath.

Whatever comes up can be received with precision and gentleness. If the experience becomes too unpleasant or painful you can use other concentrations. You can use a loving-kindness prayer or a positive visual, like still water with the moon reflecting in it. Asking myself questions can help me to stay engaged with the concentration. I will ask myself, "What if my hips are like a mountain...?" I take a few seconds to notice what arises. Then I ask, "If my heart is like the ocean...?" Again I take a few seconds before asking, "If my mind is like the sky...?" Focusing on this concentration can activate a sense of strength, flow and openness. Another question I ask is, "What if there were a little more lightness and a little more openness?" Try this and allow the inquiry to adjust your posture. These concentrations can help you experience a more positive relaxed state of being.

Do a quick lizard pushup – extend out

Over time we can build up our capacity to tolerate negative thoughts and feelings without reacting to them. I once took a seminar with a martial arts instructor. He was not big and did not look very strong. Yet he could easily take down men much bigger and more muscled than he was. He had two recommendations – first, he said we must develop a strong core. The second was – build up little by little so you can relax with the pain (I call it discomfort.) He said, "If you can tolerate the pain (discomfort) without injuring (traumatizing) your self, you can always find your way out."

I think his instruction is good for dealing with psychological and emotional discomfort as well as physical martial arts training. If I can work with myself in my mindfulness practice and learn to relax with my negative thoughts and feelings, I can find my way to a more positive part of myself.

Our inner dragons are sensitive to the level of tension we carry in our bodies. When we are tense, our dragons become tense and prepare for a struggle. Dragons can be fighters and tension is the environment that opens the door to fighting. If we can relax our muscles, think of the space outside our skin and lighten up, we change the dragon's environment. When our dragon is relaxed, we can use Discipline to find focus and clarity.

Discipline is freedom.
–Trungpa Rinpoche

The Shadow Side of Discipline

The shadow side of Discipline is becoming rigid around ones behavior. We could become angry or resentful when we are not doing our practice perfectly. When anger or resentment arises, our body tightens and our mind tightens. When our dragon feels tight we can no longer see the Big Picture, our capacity to improvise, adapt and find possibilities becomes limited. When we are rigid we limit our ability to influence ourselves – we limit our personal power.

Once we begin to relax with the unpleasant thoughts and feelings, we can begin to find our way to self-acceptance. Because we are not so tight we begin to see the Bigger Picture. There is more of a panoramic view of each situation. This panoramic view gives us much more information; there are more possible avenues of action.

Big Picture

However tight things are, you still need to have the big picture at the forefront of your mind.

—Richard Branson

Big Picture is the ability to relate to both the past and the future without getting caught in the small details. Seeing the Big Picture lets us look at the Motivation behind an action or behavior that we may not agree with. When we relax, the panorama, a wide-angle view of the situation, becomes available. We can even see multiple points of view and look at a situation from many perspectives.

Using your peripheral vision allows you to see objects around you without turning your head or moving your eyes. Your peripheral vision helps you have better balance. That is why tightrope walkers look up not down. Using their peripheral vision improves their balance.

Improved physical balance helps with emotional balance. With better physical and emotional balance we can relax and consider possibilities, solutions and opportunities.

We can see our concerns and irritations with a little more detachment, step back from ourselves, and look at the whole situation. We can *center* and summon our benevolent dragon. Centering allows us to smile at our reaction, open up, and lighten up so we can disengage from the narrow focus on our personalities habit. Seeing the Big Picture allows us to shift from the tight focus on a person's behavior to the larger question of why the other person took a particular action.

This practice changes our brain and encourages a more expansive way of looking at things. We might also be able to see

what someone outside the dynamic is seeing. What might a
more neutral person see? With more distance from the
situation, it is possible to recognize that in any exchange there
are many forces at work and usually a history that precedes any
event. When we stop and *center*, considering what factors might
be contributing to behavior, a completely different view might
arise.

One of the great things about seeing the Big Picture is that it
changes how we actually perceive reality. I think of a dragon
that can soar above and see all the parts of the story. The
dragon can see that everyone believes their own story is the only
reality.

That's what we find when we have a panoramic view: we can
see that there are many realities. Instead of believing that a
person is mean or toxic, we can see that their behavior is driven
by the need for security. I am not suggesting that we accept or
condone bad behavior. But we can be like good parents when
their child behaves badly. They make it clear that the behavior
is unacceptable and apply the appropriate consequences, but
they continue to love the child and include the child in their
personal space.

When we have a narrow focus, we can only see what is in front
of us. If we are irritated, we might make a child or another
person 'other'. This sense of separateness increases the
tendency for aggression and mean-spirited actions. Inclusion is
a powerful healer. It is the result of seeing the Big Picture.
When someone feels part of the situation, they begin to relax. It
is easier to recover our *Center* when we are not so tight. Our
benevolent dragon emerges and spreads its wings, activating a
feeling of expansiveness.

 *Uplift, expand into the space around you. Enjoy the
feeling of being open.*

The Big Picture view can help us remember that we are all in this together. When we apply the Big Picture view, we are taking a stand for inclusive personal power.

When we *center*, we remember that every person wants security. Perhaps they do not have the tools to work with their dragon and the reactive shadow is all that their dragon knows. While we may not like their behavior or agree with it, centering activates our Compassion.

The Shadow Side of Big Picture

The shadow side of the Big Picture view is getting so distracted by multiple points of view that we disconnect from what is important – from the sense of connectedness and Compassion. The new-age jargon for this is we become 'spaced out' or disassociated. We can lose our focus and no longer see ourselves on a path of cultivating personal power. When that happens, our dragon flies aimlessly, without focus or clarity. We stop attending to the Motivation, Inspiration and Discipline that are the containers for our onward journey toward a healthy personal power.

Without the Big Picture view, we will not be able to recognize that we all want to feel safe and secure; we will experience people as annoying or wrong. We will lose our ability to generate Compassion for people who have unpleasant behaviors.

Compassion

Our task must be to free ourselves by widening our circle of compassion to embrace all living creatures and the whole of nature and its beauty.

–Albert Einstein

The fundamental principle of Compassion is that everyone is trying to achieve security and avoid loss. In that way we are all the same, and we all want the same things. Yet we usually don't see that others are like us. When we see other people behave in a different way from what we think is right, we forget that they are also trying to create security for themselves and their loved ones.

I once saw a clip of a Muslim woman who was very sad because one of her sons had decided not to become a suicide bomber. From her point of view he would not be able to spend eternity in heaven and as a result he would suffer. Now, that view doesn't make sense to me from the way I see the world. It actually seems crazy — and I realize that, like me, she wants happiness for her child. She wants her child not to suffer. So, although I don't like what she wants for her child and I disagree strongly with her view, I can have Compassion for her sadness. It doesn't mean I agree with her or condone what she does, but it does mean that I don't have to reject her as a human being. Instead, I can reject her behavior as something I don't think is right.

I find the most immediate way to generate a feeling of Compassion is to think of someone who represents it to me. One of the practices I use is to think of Mother Teresa. Originally named Agnes, she chose to be named after another archetype, Theresa of Lisieux, the "little" Theresa who wrote, "I applied myself especially to practice little virtues, not having the facility to preform great ones..." From this came Mother Teresa's famous quote, "We cannot all do great things. But we can do small things with great love."

Learning about Mother Teresa and her journey, her capacity to see the good in people, has allowed me to rehabilitate a quality of goodness in myself. To be clear, you don't have to use a famous archetype; your model for Compassion might be a friend, some words, a place or even an animal that triggers the feeling in you.

Whatever it is that opens your heart, even for a second, is worth doing over and over again. Each time your neural pathway for Compassion has ping, it strengthens your capacity for kindness. When I think of my Compassionate dragon I imagine it is sheltering me, holding me in its generous, warm arms. I imagine this dragon smiling, kindly radiating light.

What is your Compassion dragon like?

Compassion contains qualities such as kindness, perseverance, warmth and resolve. Trungpa Rinpoche used the term 'basic goodness' to describe what I believe is our natural tendency of altruism. The cultivation of Compassion is like diamond mining. It can take sifting through a huge roomful of dirt to get a handful of diamonds. The diamonds of Compassion are there, as is our basic goodness. Uncovering the Compassion that lies within each of us is a process of patience and perseverance and technique. It takes practice, kindness and perseverance to awaken our Compassionate dragon.

Once again, mindfulness can help. When we sit quietly and observe our mind we become aware of our habits of thinking. We notice that we think the same kinds of thoughts over and over again, typically thoughts related to judging, planning, desiring and worrying. We can see that these thoughts are an attempt to escape discomfort. Planning is a way to feel safe because it imagines a known outcome. Judging is a way to feel that we are secure because we are right. Desiring keeps us from feeling anxious, and worrying allows us to prepare for future problems.

When we recognize that we are using these habits of thinking to escape the reality of the moment, we can invite Compassion for ourselves. Instead of continuing along the story of habitual thoughts, we can use the centering process to return to the present moment.

The Shadow Side of Compassion

As with the other aspects, however, there's a shadow side of Compassion. For example, the phrase 'compassion burn out,' is familiar in the world of caregiving. Caregiving can be rewarding and fulfilling – and utterly exhausting. For caregivers, the struggle to manifest Compassion and love while acknowledging fear, financial stress, and guilt can be challenging.

We can limit or avoid experiencing Compassion burnout by using the element of Discipline. We can create time to look after ourselves, rest, eat healthy food, exercise and spend time with friends and family, or in nature. Centering and inviting Inspiration helps to give us access to more energy and Compassion. In turn, Compassion is the precursor to Confidence, which is the final piece of our personal power process.

 Uplift your posture, exhale and think of something that makes you smile.

Confidence

When you have confidence, you can have a lot of fun. And when you have fun, you can do amazing things.

— Joe Namath

Usually what keeps us from showing up as powerful, influential and effective is fear. Our personality constructs strategies to protect us. Fear of loss keeps those strategies in place. We worry that, if we take powerful action, things might get out of control. If we speak truth to power others might not like us or, even worse, say disparaging things about us. If we act because we know in our bones we are right, people might not agree, resistance might turn violent and someone could get hurt.

It takes Confidence to face our fear: Confidence that our Motivation is more important than our safety and Confidence that our Inspiration will continue to nourish our vision. We need to feel confident that our Discipline will strengthen our capacity to stay with our practice, allow us to see the Big Picture and help us remember that we are connected even when we feel threatened. To cultivate Compassion when others behave in mean-spirited ways takes Confidence in the belief of basic goodness.

Confidence is the underlying quality for responsibility. When we are *centered*, responsibility helps to drive our actions.

As Lama Yeshe Rinpoche wrote, "Most people want to be free but don't want to take responsibilities. But freedom is inseparable from responsibility! If I have the freedom to think, it is my responsibility to think positively. If I have the freedom to speak, it is my responsibility to speak properly and meaningfully. If I have the freedom to act, it is my responsibility to act correctly. Nobody else can take that decision for me."

What does a confident dragon look like and act like? Coming from my martial arts experience, I imagine a calm, benevolent warrior. I think of Nelson Mandela, Morihei Ueshiba, the founder of Aikido, and a lion looking out over the savanna. What images and archetypes arise for you when you think of Confidence?

 Lengthen your spine, expand out, ask, "What if there was a little more confidence?"

Confidence can also be thought of as belief. Bruce Lipton's book, *The Biology of Belief*, points to how the power of belief can affect our body's health and our capacity to act in the world. Positive belief allows us to move beyond our fears. The fear may still be present and we can Discipline ourselves to practice focusing more on the positive beliefs than on our doubts. We can use the 'yes – and' technique, 'yes I am afraid – *and* I believe that speaking truth to power is more important than being safe.'

Some years ago I made a cape for a client to wear to increase her confidence. It is made of heavy velvet and if you are not too tall it will drag on the ground behind you. The weight opens your chest, broadens your shoulders and brings them down away from your ears. This is the body shaping itself in the mode of Confidence. As the muscle groups change, from tight and closed to open and relaxed, different chemicals are released. As these chemicals change the brain and different thoughts arise, the story changes. The sense of having a weight down your back can make you feel supported from behind. The story changes from being alone to being supported.

There are people who want you to succeed in your activities. Imagine their warm hands on your back supporting you. Imagine their smiling faces. Let that support fill you with confidence.

The Shadow – Over Confidence

As always it is important to be on the lookout for the shadow side – over-confidence. If we become over-confident we lose our capacity to receive feedback. We can lose our humility and forget that our actions are for the benefit of something larger than ourselves. Big Picture and Compassion become obscured by self-serving and grandiose behaviors.

I once said, "The best gift you can give someone is to get yourself together." Unless we are able to manage our unskillful reactions to unpleasant circumstances, we won't be able to bring positive influence to the conversations and interactions we have with others. The will and the skill to effect positive change is predicated on our ability to harness the power of our inner dragons.

> *When you are clearly competent, you can engage the other people in a way that increases their commitment and confidence.*

> –Mette Norgaard

Effecting positive change is the purview of Social Power. Like Personal Power, Social Power has aspects or elements that increase our positive influence on conversations and interactions.

PART 3

Dragon Power is Influence

It would be difficult to exaggerate the degree to which we are influenced by those we influence.

—Eric Hoffer

CHAPTER 5

Social Power, Influencing Others

POWER - your capacity to make a difference in the world by influencing the states of other people.

—Voss, Chris; Raz, Tahl

Dragon energy is noticeable; it is difficult to ignore a person when their dragon power is activated. Dragon power is influence, and influence is the effect one person has on another.

We are continually influencing and being influenced by others. It is said that at least seventy percent of communication is non-verbal. We affect each other because we are connected. As the German writer Johann Wolfgang von Goethe said, "In nature we never see anything as isolated, but everything in connection with something else which is before it, beside it, under it and over it."

Neuroscience has been exploring this phenomena, using the terms 'mirror neurons' and 'limbic resonance' to explain what happens in the brain and body that makes us so sensitive to each other. I invite you to think about your own experiences of being affected by people non-verbally. Have you ever seen someone eat something you find repulsive and found your body recoiling? Have you seen someone tenderly holding a baby, a puppy or a kitten and felt a softness and warmth in your body?

Our sense of self is usually organized in terms of our own thoughts and feelings. But other people's sense of who we are comes from how they perceive our energy, the quality of our vitality and intensity. People can have a sense of who we are even if they can't see our face. Have you ever noticed the way someone is sitting or standing and had a strong feeling of attraction or repulsion toward them even if you couldn't see their face? That's because we respond to people on an energetic level, even without words or facial expression. We are being influenced and influencing others all the time.

There are factors that increase our capacity to influence others and manage the way we are influenced by others. These factors are Size, Warmth, Resilience, Connection, Knowledge and Intuition. The first factor we will explore is Size.

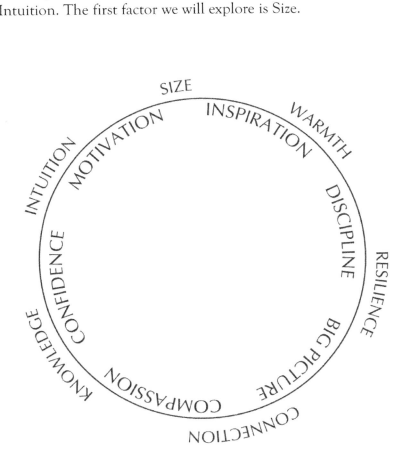

Size

My presence speaks volumes before I say a word

—Mos Def

I think of dragons as having big energy. The dragon within me wants to feel big and empowered. It wants to feel free to fly, to sing, to speak what is in my heart.

In terms of influencing people, especially in the world of organizations, one thing that has become clear to me is that Size matters. It's not the Size of your biceps or how tall you are but the Size of your spirit that makes people notice you. In this case, Size refers to a person's presence, their energy and intensity.

When a person has big energy, when they expand and include others, they are more influential. We notice people with big energy, and they have an effect on us. Alexander the Great, Mother Teresa and the founder of Aikido, Morhei Ueshiba, were only five feet tall, yet no one would think of them as small. They were impressively powerful and influential.

I have coached people with multiple PhDs. They are often the smartest people in the room, and yet some of them don't have much of a voice. Because their presence is small, other people cannot feel them and so they become invisible. Perhaps you can think of an experience when you have been in a meeting or with a group and someone calls on a person you had not noticed before. A person who has a small presence may have the most insightful or brilliant idea, but their idea will not become accessible because they don't have enough of a presence to be heard.

Conversely, a person might, be ignorant or obtuse and yet everyone in the room hears their views. That person might dominate the discussion because they are expansive and have a way of displaying their expansiveness, which makes them more visible and influential than their counterparts.

Growing Your Presence Takes Practice

For many people, developing a big presence is a practice. Some of us were given explicit instructions as children to keep our energy small, told to be ladylike, to be quiet – to be seen and not heard. In some cultures, children are specifically taught not to be big. For example, in Asia, the message, particularly for women, is typically, 'Keep your energy tucked in, don't let your energy touch other people in public.' At home it may be an entirely different matter; the women may rule the house and once inside the walls they can transform into energetic giants.

In their book, *Stealing Fire*, Steven Kotler and Jamie Wheal pointed out that "Transformational leaders not only regulated their own nervous systems better than most; they also regulated other people's. In the same way that multiple clocks on a wall end up synchronizing to the one with the biggest pendulum, emergent leaders can entrain their entire teams and create a powerful group flow experience." Transformational leaders are influential actors in the world of organizations. It takes energy and a big presence to influence change in individuals and social systems.

Make your presence bigger now – uplift your posture and extend your arms out.

Our Environment Affects Our Size

It is thought that goldfish grow only to the Size of their enclosure. Bonsai trees grow only to the Size of the pot they are placed in. I believe that as humans, we too are affected by the Size of the environment we spend time in.

I once had a black belt visitor come to my Aikido dojo (a martial arts place of training), and take a class with me. It turns out he was also a teacher and had an Aikido school in Southern California. As I watched his movement I noticed that he had a very big, expansive presence. Most Aikido teachers do, because a dojo is usually a large space and the teacher is used to filling that space with his or her presence. But I noticed that my visitor did not have much energy above his head. I asked whether his dojo had a low ceiling. "Why yes," he exclaimed, " How do you know that?" My answer was that his energy was wide and not high. Like a goldfish or a bonsai, his energy had grown to fill the Size of the enclosure he was working in.

Not only can spending time in big spaces create a tendency to have a big presence, the Size of a person's presence can change with a changing context. If you see someone you would like to avoid you will try to make yourself seem small in hopes that they will not notice you. Athletes, no matter what their physical Size, seem big, even huge, on the field or the court – their energy fills the space where they are playing. Then you see them in an interview or in a social situation and they have made their presence smaller. They have adjusted their presence to adapt to what they feel is appropriate in that environment. In business, the notion of being promoted to a more powerful position is associated with getting a larger office. To practice increasing my Size I imagine my benevolent dragon, wings spread behind me. As I settle into the image, I feel more expansive – bigger, taller and wider.

Our Presence is Like a Bubble Around Us

The way we experience ourselves and the way other people experience us does not stop at our skin. There is a whole part of our being that lives outside of our skin. We carry our 'bubble' of self around with us. According to neuroscientists who have been examining this phenomenon, the brain seems to construct multiple representations of space. These representations include personal, peripersonal, and extra-personal space. *Personal space* refers to the space occupied by the body; *peripersonal space* refers to space surrounding our body within the reach of our arms and legs; and *extra-personal space* refers to space beyond the reach of our limbs.

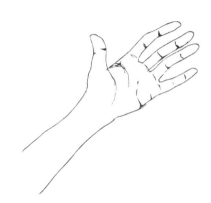

My personal experience is that we can learn to grow our extra-personal space, which we need to do if we want to be influential. One method is simply to sit and stand up straighter, not in a stiff way, but in an uplifted way. Also, it is important to extend your arms out instead of folding or crossing them. Folding and crossing your arms activates your flexor muscles, which pulls energy in. Folded arms also sends a message that you are shutting others out. Extending your arms in an open gesture allows energy to flow outward, sending a message of inclusion, a 'we are in this together' message.

Sit up a little straighter, extend your arms and fingers, let your presence fill the room.

As Barbara Tversky wrote in *Mind in Motion: How Action Shapes Thought*, "Put simply, gestures change thought. The trick is to create gestures that establish a space of ideas that represents the thought felicitously. That gestures have the power to change thought has powerful implications for communication, in the classroom and outside. Words can be and all too often are ambiguous, even words describing something as basic as space, the surroundings we carry with us at all times. Gestures, by contrast, are explicit."

If your gestures are open rather than closed and your energy is expansive rather than small, you will be noticed and you will have a voice. This doesn't mean that people will agree with you – but it does mean that they will hear you.

The Dark Side of the Size Dragon

The shadow side of Size is that when we know people see us as a powerful force it becomes easy to bully them, to lay our trip on them so to speak. If we are not aware, we can create a divisive environment by criticizing or even belittling them. We might begin to believe the story that we are always right and people should do what we say. If we lose our humility and our sense of wonder, we are on a slippery slope to believing that we are better than others. If our patience and compassion are reduced, then what arises in their place is righteousness and incisiveness, our shadow dragon.

We should always be on the lookout for signs that we have lost our way. Asking friends or mentors for feedback can be helpful.

I believe we can grow a culture of people who have big energy and use it for uniting rather than dividing communities. As long as we are warm and inclusive, our power can be used to support and not to dominate.

Rub your hands together for a few seconds. Straighten your arms and feel the tingling in your hands. Imagine lights in your fingers are shining on the walls.

Warmth

When you are gentle and warm, you can shake the world.

—Mahatma Gandhi

Protector dragons have strong qualities of Warmth and gentleness. When we activate our protector dragon, we feel the power of affection and care for people, animals and nature. If we have worked with our dragon and learned how to contain and redirect the wildness within all that power and intensity, we will notice a Warmth and tenderness. Warmth is a powerful influencer. There is a sense of surrender, of being drawn in, like being in love.

When a person is warm, others feel accepted and included; as a result, they become more receptive to suggestion. This is because of mirror neurons. According to Barbara Tversky, "The mirror system mediates and reflects just about every kind of action: of our hands, our legs, our posture, our faces. The mimicking is internal, but it can leak out into actual behavior. We imitate each other's body movements and facial expressions. Mirroring means that the bodies of others get internalized in our minds and our bodies get internalized in theirs."

When people feel the Warmth and affection we radiate, their own Warmth and affection begins to activate, which releases the hormone oxytocin. Oxytocin has two primary effects: it reduces anxiety about one another and motivates us to cooperate. Oxytocin also modulates dopamine, the brain's reward and motivational reinforcement chemical. Generally oxytocin release is reciprocal; if our interaction causes your brain to make oxytocin, it will usually do the same for mine. We both begin to relax, which eases any tension and allows our systems to tune into each other.

Be careful not to mistake Warmth for weakness. It is far from weak – Warmth has an impressive capacity to create influence, as this quote from *The Book of Joy* by Douglas Abrams will attest. "As I sat next to the Dalai Lama I could feel in his posture and his body language the power of a leader. I remembered how strongly and tenderly he had held my hand the first time we met. His kindness did not in any way diminish his power, a valuable reminder that compassion is a feature of strength, not weakness, a point they would make throughout our conversations."

It is important to be clear that accepting a person does not mean that you accept their behavior. As I mentioned in the section on Compassion, it is important to separate the behavior from the person. Just as in good parenting, we want to make it clear that we love the child and sometimes not the behavior. So with adults, if we want to increase our positive power, we need to cultivate Warmth — even toward those that we disagree with.

In *Never Split the Difference*, Chris Voss and Raz Tahl say, "When we radiate warmth and acceptance, conversations just seem to flow. When we enter a room with a level of comfort and enthusiasm, we attract people toward us. Smile at someone on the street, and as a reflex they'll smile back. Understanding that reflex and putting it into practice is critical to the success of just about every negotiating skill there is to learn."

Conversely when a person shows up with strength but without Warmth they will use domination rather than collaboration as a strategy to get their way. Domination separates the leader from others in the meeting or the conversation. If a leader is without Warmth, people become tense or withdrawn. Conversations might stall because people stop listening to each other. It becomes more difficult to move projects forward and work toward resolution.

Inspiration Can Help to Cultivate a Habit of Warmth

Cultivating a habit of Warmth takes practice. I use the principles from the Inspiration aspect of my personal power practice. I think of people, things or places that make me want to smile: my grandchildren playing and laughing, inspiring moments in nature, how it felt to be in the presence of the Dalai Lama. I touch into these concentrations throughout the day for a few seconds here or a minute there. We have a Leadership Embodiment centering app and I have set times on my phone to remind me to *Center* during the day. I have to practice constantly because if I don't, I get sucked into the day's headlines or concern about a project that may not be going well. It's a percentage game – how much time do I spend on irritations and concerns verses the time I spend connecting to moments that make me smile.

 Take a few seconds to invite a feeling of strength in your back and tenderness in your heart. Think of something that makes you smile.

Watch for the Approval Trap

Like all behaviors, cultivating Warmth and affection has a shadow side. The shadow is falling into the approval trap, becoming so attached to wanting people to like you that you compromise your values or ethics to win someone's approval. Trying to get a promotion or forming a relationship with someone who is attractive or powerful can lead to behaviors that we may regret.

Finding a way to have Warmth and be inclusive without compromising our truth takes awareness. We need to check in with ourselves when we realize that we really want a person or group of people to like and admire us. We need to ask ourselves, "Are we getting too attached to the outcome?" That kind of daily introspection can keep us from compromising our integrity.

The Warmth and gentleness of our protector dragon activates a feeling of lightness and buoyancy. When there is no heaviness, more energy is available and we find ourselves being more Resilient and positive.

Resilience

Courage is going from failure to failure without losing enthusiasm.

—Winston Churchill

My benevolent dragon is Resilient. Training my dragon has allowed me to channel the power in a more skillful way so the dragon energy can be used to keep going and not give up when things become difficult.

Resilience is a word that I hear frequently as we try to manage fast-paced and complicated schedules. We are constantly 'on'; we have meetings while driving and 'working lunches' and we are wedded to our devices. Resilience implies bouncing back from a draining or negative experience; it implies being upbeat and cheerful in the face of challenges. So how do we keep from being depleted, exhausted and overwhelmed?

I think there are two major components to Resilience – the first is tapping into our *centered* self so we are allowing the energy to *come through us*. We are open and in flow, not forcing or over exerting at the task. When we are in our *centered* state we have access to the zone or flow-state. I find it helps to imagine that the flow is like a breeze at my back, helping me move through the day with ease.

Sense the wind at your back supporting you.

When I feel stuck I call on my 'posse', I use Einstein or the Dali Lama to activate qualities of creativity. I can connect to Compassion and open my heart when I think of laughing with my grandchildren.

When I feel anxious or nervous I remember the moment when I first saw Nelson Mandela and felt the power and courage he radiated after so many years in prison. Taking the time to focus on inspiring archetypes connects me to the part of myself that has those qualities. It allows me to shift my state of being to my more creative, compassionate and courageous self. I feel more Resilient and capable of inspired action.

 Remember the feeling of a wind at your back for a moment. Imagine people who love you have their hands on your back, sense the support and energy, invite compassion and courage to flow through you.

The second component of Resilience is connected to the first – it is not being attached to the results. It is stressful and tiring to feel like we have to achieve a specific outcome within a certain time frame. We become tense when we experience resistance, and rather than taking a breath and reassessing the situation, we push ourselves to complete the task. It is exhausting to work this way and to feel that we have to do it by ourselves.

Growing up most of us heard admonishments like, "No one will do it for you", "It is up to you" and "You are responsible." We were never told that there is a wonderful state of being often called the 'zone' or 'flow state' in which we feel helped and supported and can accomplish activities with relative ease. To tap this wonderful state of being we need to pay attention to the part of ourselves that lies outside our skin. We need to summon our benevolent dragon and invite the dragon force to flow through us.

Adapting to changing circumstances is key to being Resilient. When we *Center* and remember we are interconnected we feel less alone and isolated; we can relax and tolerate things not going well. We can see a bigger view of the situation and we have more access to creative solutions. We are also more able to influence a situation when we radiate a sense of Resilience. People are attracted to Resilience; consciously or unconsciously the mirror principle is at work and they recognize that someone else's Resilience affects them.

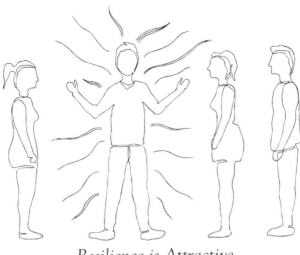

Resilience is Attractive

We Learn from Failure

Not being attached to the outcome implies that failure is an option – we might not accomplish our goal in the way we would like. It is not easy to accept that failure is always a possibility because we have been educated to believe that we must succeed and we must do everything ourselves.

When we are Resilient, we are more able to accept failure. In his wonderful book, *The Art of Learning*, Josh Waizkins said, "Resilience is the ability to reorient relationship to fear, discomfort and suffering. There is a beauty in pain and fear because there is a great opportunity to learn."

There are many inspirational people who succeeded because they failed a lot –Elon Musk and Michael Jordan come to mind. You don't have to do your work all alone, you have a benevolent dragon to call upon. Remember you are Noble, Awesome and Shiny.

Not being attached to the outcome and practicing inviting support takes Discipline. The good news is that it can be done in twenty seconds, five seconds or one second.

 Imagine you are porous – actually our atoms are mostly space. Invite people or things that represent wisdom, compassion and courage to flow through you.

Keeping Ourselves Accountable

Pressure is a privilege

—Billy Jean King

And then there is the shadow to Resilience. The shadow is too much forward momentum without time for feedback or reflection. It is possible to laminate optimism over real concerns and potential problems. Sometimes it is important to listen to the naysayers, to take the time to consider their point of view. We may need to slow down and weigh the consequences of failure and think about how much failure is tolerable in the situation.

As always, receiving feedback, awareness and reflection are important so we can keep from slipping into the shadow when we are acting in a powerful, influential way. It is worthwhile to reflect and wonder on a daily basis if we are slipping into attachment to outcome. We should question if we believe that we alone are responsible for success or failure. The cultural

habit of thinking that we must make things happen is strong in
us. It will take Discipline to remember to connect to our
centered self, our resourceful self, and the wisdom, courage and
Compassion that are always there.

Connection

*When we try to pick out anything by itself, we find it hitched
to everything else in the universe.*

–John Muir

The connector dragon has a good grasp of the language, context
and history of the situation. Sometimes the connector dragon is
overcome with enthusiasm and offers too many ideas and
possibilities. So it is important to call upon the personal power
of discipline to manage the energy of an enthusiastic connector
dragon.

Connecters know how to bring people together. They are able
to connect people with ideas and create circumstances that
allow possibilities to unfold and projects to flourish.
Connection is often referred to as something you do–"to
connect." I prefer to think of Connection as a noun, something
that exists and does not need an activity to appear. From this
point of view we are already connected. Connection is not
something we do; it is something we are, even without language.
We affect each other all the time; studies on mirror neurons
and limbic resonance have shown that one person can change
another's perception just by being in proximity to them.

In their inspiring book, *The Art of Possibility*, Rosamund and
Benjamin Zander describe what they call the WE story as a way
of clarifying the organic nature of connection. "The WE story
defines a human being in a specific way: It says we are our
central selves seeking to contribute, naturally engaged, forever
in a dance with each other. It points to relationship rather than
to individuals, to communication patterns, gestures and
movement rather than to discrete objects and identities. It
attests to the in-between. Like the particle and wave nature of
light, the WE is both a living entity and a long line of

development unfolding. This new being, the WE of us, comes into view as we look for it – the vital entity of our company or community or group of two. Then the protagonist of our story, the entity called WE, steps forward and takes on a life of its own."

Connection is a power that all of us have and only some of us use. As the Zanders point out, when we begin to look for something we often see that it was always there. When we have confidence that we are all connected, we can relax and naturally engage in conversations. We can point out possibilities and encourage actions. We don't have to convince 'them' because whoever they are, they are not separate from us. We can be at ease and say what we need to say, allowing whatever the response is to land in the space between us. To do that, we can apply the 'Listening from *Center*' practice.

When using *centered* listening, we let critical or unpleasant words land in the space or on the table in front of us. Usually we internalize a criticism and feel annoyed or hurt by negative assertions. Putting the words in the space lets us look at them from a distance. When we let what is said land in the space between us, and invite Inspiration, we usually are less reactive, more able to keep conversations going and move toward better resolutions.

Recognizing that we are connected to everything allows us to gain insights and experience subtle shifts in relationships, especially in the non-verbal realm. It's worth repeating John Muir's quote, "When we try to pick out anything by itself, we find it hitched to everything else in the universe."

Uplift and expand out, the space connects to everything, seeing the shapes of the space between objects and people relaxes the mind and puts you in a state of connection.

There is Power in Space

An important and difficult concept to grasp is our Connection to space. In western culture, space is not usually thought of as a resource. It is considered to be something that is empty of activity as in, 'there was lots of space in the locker room because few people were there', or something that can be filled, as in 'there was lots of space on the wall for paintings'.

Recently the Chinese system of geomancy, feng shui, has become more popular. It relates to the 'invisible forces' surrounding objects and how they interact in the space. Organizing the way objects are placed in space is thought to harmonize individuals with their surrounding environment. Feng shui practitioners feel it is important to have the right placement of objects in the space surrounding them.

As artists know well, there is a power in space. French composer Claude Debussy said, "The music is the spaces between the notes". People who work in design know there is an intelligent self-organizing principle in the space. We all use this principle when we drive a car. When we drive well, we organize around the spaces, not the other cars. Focusing on the other cars can make us nervous. Focusing on the space between the cars can help us stay calm and drive more smoothly.

Connecting to Space Enhances Your Timing

Timing is the skill involved in doing something at the precise moment for optimum effect. Our Connection to the space can give us better timing. In many activities timing is considered to be the most important aspect of accomplishing an action. We all know that you can say the right thing at the wrong time and ruin a wonderful opportunity.

When I practice aikido I have learned not to look at my partner when he is attacking me. Instead I use 'soft eyes' and focus on the space. When I do this I have better timing, which is crucial when practicing martial arts. If I do look at my partner or the strike, I tense up and my timing is thrown off.

When I am in a meeting or talking to someone and I remember that the space around us connects us, my conversational timing is better. I become a better listener and don't talk as fast or feel that I have to convince the other person to agree with me.

 Put your attention on the space around you for a few seconds.

The Dark Side: Information Overload

The darker side of Connection is pushing too much information on people and not allowing a natural flow. In the United States we use the acronym TMI, meaning 'too much information' to describe the experience of being overwhelmed by the amount of information in a conversation, text or email. Often the person overdoing the connection is actually trying to offer support and doesn't realize that the recipient is shutting down because they can't take in so much information at one time. It's like trying to communicate with someone who doesn't speak the same language. If the person being spoken to doesn't seem to understand, the speaker might raise their voice in an attempt to connect. Sadly, that usually has the opposite effect, causing the listener to withdraw.

Connection is what links us to each other and to the space around us. The quality of this Connection can be enhanced when we are interested in learning about the world around us. One way we learn is that we seek Knowledge.

Knowledge

I'm hungry for knowledge. The whole thing is to learn every day, to get brighter and brighter. That's what this world is about. You look at someone like Gandhi, and he glowed. Martin Luther King glowed. Muhammad Ali glowed. I think that's from being bright all the time, and trying to be brighter.

–Jay-Z

Having Knowledge can create respect and can help clarify and focus what needs to be done. We can be helpful and support projects and ideas. When we are insecure our knowledge becomes more of a know-it-all, trying to show people how smart it is in order to gain their approval. Or our insecurity can drive us to hoard information, giving the impression we know things and will exact a price for sharing the information.

There are several types of Knowledge that are used to influence outcomes. Explicit Knowledge is communicating information that is clear and exact. Implicit Knowledge is information that suggests an idea without directly expressing it. Tacit Knowledge is information that is understood or implied without being stated.

Explicit Knowledge

Explicit Knowledge is having a good grasp of the language, context and history of the situation. Having explicit Knowledge can help to bring clarity and precision to what is happening and what needs to be done.

Being an expert is an example of explicit Knowledge. An expert is someone who has a comprehensive and authoritative Knowledge or skill in a particular area. Generally we expect an expert to be reliable and accurate. Facts, figures, numbers and data all imply that there is a correct way to understand the situation. When a person exhibits this type of Knowledge, it elicits respect, which is a powerful position to exert influence on situations.

Implicit Knowledge

Another type of Knowledge is implicit Knowledge. Implicit Knowledge is the practical application of Knowledge. Implicit refers to something that is suggested or implied, but never clearly said. It has the power of implying or suggesting something in addition to what is explicit. An example would be, " There was an implicit agreement not to raise the subject." Another way to think about it is that explicit is the 'know-what' and implicit is the 'know-how'. In order for Knowledge to be influential and powerful, both explicit and implicit communications need to be employed.

Tacit Knowledge

For many people explicit and implicit types of Knowledge are more believable and attractive than tacit Knowledge. Tacit Knowledge is the knowing of things without being able to explain how you know – like riding a bicycle. Reading about how to ride a bicycle or watching a video describing how to ride a bicycle does not really help you learn to ride a bicycle. I have worked with some leaders who had an uncanny ability to influence their team to find solutions where none were apparent. I have seen managers that can see how and when to implement deliverables; so the client feels confident and committed, allowing projects to move forward smoothly. If you ask them how they do it they will not be able to give a definitive answer.

One way of increasing our influence, and therefore our power, is to find ways to make tacit Knowledge explicit. It can be done. All great coaches are in the business of helping the person or people they are coaching to move from 'know what' – understanding what to do – to 'know how', being able to actually perform the activity successfully. Coaches and facilitators need to be able to break down the process into small increments in order for the knowledge to move from the cognitive system – the mind, to the limbic system – the body. Once the Knowledge is in the body a person can perform the activity, even in a situation of low-grade threat.

How well a person performs the activity is related to the amount of practice that a person engages in – as Houdini said, "Magic is Practice." Training our dragon to shift from 'know what' to 'know how' takes practice.

 Practice now; inhale and uplift, expand out and think of something that makes you smile.

Having access to explicit Knowledge, implicit Knowledge and tacit Knowledge gives us greater capacity to influence a situation. Yet knowledge by itself is not enough to change people's states of being. The smartest people are often not the most influential or seen as powerful. Knowledge is just one piece in a larger framework of power.

The Shadow Side of Knowledge

Let us not overlook the shadow side of Knowledge. The shadow is dominating the conversation so it becomes a monologue rather than a dialogue. It is easy to start believing that you are right when you have credentials touting your accomplishments. Sometimes experts fall into an attitude of superiority believing that they are better than those who have not earned similar credentials. It is easy to forget that we are all learners and that science and research are constantly changing. What is "true and real" is often "true and real" only for a time. People used to believe the world was flat, and some still do believe that. Not long ago it was said by doctors that heart conditions could not be reversed. Now the Intensive Cardiac Rehabilitation (ICR) network is growing rapidly, including national partnerships with Medicare and many health insurance companies, including Anthem Blue Cross/Blue Shield.

Knowledge is an impressive human capacity and if used with Compassion and inclusion can be a tool to empower people and cultures. And yet it is still only a piece of the whole that allows a person to live in their power. Another piece is Intuition.

Intuition

Intuition will tell the thinking mind where to look next.
—Jonas Salk

Intuition is the hidden form of Knowledge – Knowledge that can't be explained by data, facts or figures. It is as if we have an intuitive dragon that is alive and well in us. It is the part that knows what is right or true and what needs to be done in a given situation. The Intuitive dragon doesn't always make rational sense, so we usually don't listen and tend to ignore it. We've been taught to be rational and logical — and of course dragons are mythical, so why would we listen to them? Yet, if we want access to our full power, we need to learn how to listen to our Intuitive dragon's voice.

Intuition arises from our limbic system, the much older and less rational part of our brain that is responsible for our moods and emotions. The newest part of our brain, the neo-cortex, loves to think and reason. But our limbic system is a more instinctive part of us, more geared toward Connection and relationship than toward facts and figures.

Some consider Intuition to be a type of Knowledge. Although that is a valid way of looking at it, I prefer to view Intuition as having a separate set of influences that put it in its own power category.

Being Intuitive is an influential characteristic that imbues a person with an aura of power. Highly rational people are often quite impressed and somewhat mystified by highly Intuitive people. Yet many of the great scientists and inventors have acknowledged that it was Intuition that led them to their discovery or insight. As Jonas Salk implies, there is a state of being that precedes the state of cognitive knowing.

Take a breath and ask your intuition, " What would it be like if there was a little more ease? Wait and see what arises."

When we speak about Intuition some people might point to the psychiatrist Carl Jung's collective unconscious. Some describe Intuition as a spirit guide or angel, while for others it is a felt sense or a gut feeling. Whatever the doorway, Intuition somehow lets us find information from a part of ourselves that lies outside our rational thinking.

Years ago I wrote a book called *The Intuitive Body*, in which I discussed types of Intuition and ways people could train their Intuition to be more accurate and helpful. My premise was then and is still that we are all equally Intuitive. The difference is that some people can separate Intuitive information from projections or ideas of what a person is experiencing based on their fears and desires. Still others let their concerns and irritations ride roughshod over their Intuition.

Three Kinds of Intuition

It takes practice is to separate Intuitive knowing from our fears and desires. I am deeply grateful to Helen Palmer, author of a number of Enneagram books, for pointing this out. Helen Palmer articulated the three kinds of Intuition: clairvoyance – clear seeing; clairaudience – clear hearing; and clairsentience – clear feeling.

In all three kinds of Intuition, the practice is to correctly interpret what you are seeing, hearing or feeling. It is important not to project your fears and desires onto your experience. When people receive distorted information and act on it, they can create unnecessary problems for their family, their team or their organization.

On the other hand, when information is not tainted by fears and desires, the possibilities are endless. Inviting your Intuitive dragon to consider solutions and connections that are beyond what is considered rational and culturally accepted can push the envelope of what is not considered possible and lead to innovation.

The Dark Dragon of Intuition

The shadow side of Intuition is being sort of right. 'Sort of right' is so detrimental because you might give information that is close enough to the truth to be believable and far enough away to create damage – as when people follow bad advice and end up making destructive mistakes.

Ideally the Intuitive person is merely a conduit for Intuitive information, not making up a story. Giving misleading information and calling it Intuition is an inappropriate use of power. To use Intuition skillfully we must be honest with ourselves and be careful not to project our own fears and desires on to others.

Now that we have explored how to summon our Dragon Power and engage the aspects of Personal Power, we can increase our capacity for living our lives fully.

We can use the surges of dragon energy to create beauty and flow in our lives. We know how to rouse our benevolent dragon and use the aspects of Social Power to more skillfully influence others and manage the way we are influenced by others.

So let's do it.....

PART 4

Making It Happen

Knowing is not enough; we must apply. Willing is not enough; we must do.

—Johann Wolfgang von Goethe

CHAPTER 6

Now is the Time to Summon Our Power

With great Power comes great Responsibility

—Spider Man

Now is the time to summon our power, to speak truth to power, to act on behalf of others – to bring wisdom, compassion and creativity to the personal and global challenges that affect everyone on this planet.

Taking responsibility for what we can do motivates us to use our power skillfully.

We need to be able to implement and sustain our intention in order to serve for the greater good. There will be challenges along the way; we may have to deal with being in the spotlight and the unwanted attention and assumptions that may be thrust upon us. Learning to use and not abuse our power is a whole life practice.

We can call upon our benevolent dragon to help us answer the call. We have the knowhow and the tools, so let's do it.

Implementing

In our context, implementing means the ability to use concrete measures to carry out an activity or accomplish something.

Talking about what needs to be done is not the same as doing it. To initiate action involves timing and focus. As I mentioned in the chapter on Connection our timing is better when we open up and connect into the space. It helps to take a moment to *Center* and tune into the situation before acting. When we are *centered* we are able to perceive the right moment to initiate an action. We are more effective when we initiate at the right time.

 Lengthen your spine, soften your chest and open up by focusing on the space in the room.

To get momentum to act we need Motivation and Inspiration so we can tap into the importance of taking action and speaking up. We need to rouse ourselves, to call upon our power dragon, for the energy and resolve to continue acting on behalf of the people and projects we want to support without exhausting ourselves and burning out.

In Leadership Embodiment we use the shape and focus of a triangle to energize the activity. We use analogies like the bow of a boat, the stance of an archer, or the blade of a knife to communicate the capacity to easily move through resistance.

Move through resistance with ease

Our boat needs to be big enough carry all the passengers involved. It doesn't matter whether the project is the size of a family or a country; the key is to include everyone. The focus and grace of an archer ready to loose an arrow gives us the Confidence that we can move straight toward our goals. Just as a sharp knife can cut smoothly without aggression, we can find a way to skillfully navigate resistance, and we can do it with optimism and Warmth.

It is helpful to make a plan with clear intentions. For instance I usually begin by thinking about a project, then make notes to help clarify my ideas. Next, I might discuss my ideas with friends or colleagues. Discussing my plan helps to activate my passion and increase my excitement. It is important to be aware of potential obstacles or issues that may arise.

Fifty Percent Mastery and Fifty Percent Mystery

It helps to have a plan, but we must be careful to not be attached to it because implementing doesn't always go smoothly. For that reason, I believe that it is important to welcome the mystery. In fact I would go as far as to say that we can operate with fifty percent mastery and fifty percent mystery. No matter how well we train our dragon there will always be some mystery regarding how things unfold. There are unexpected twists and turns that surface in any endeavor. I can't always understand why some thoughts or feelings arise. I am amazed at how quickly we can surprise ourselves with a sudden flash of insight or an unexpected flush of anger. The mastery is to recover our *centered* state as soon as possible and resume our activities with Resilience and Inspiration.

As Mingyur Rinpoche wrote, *Confidence cannot mature without the acceptance of uncertainty.*

To implement our plans, we need to draw on our practice to call up our Noble, Awesome and Shiny dragon. Our positive dragon will help us contain our passion and focus our strength and grace as we engage with life. The next challenge is to sustain this Inspiration and use our Resilience to not give up.

Sustaining

I find it interesting that we can so easily sustain negative habits like obsessing over something we want or someone we don't like, eating unhealthy food, or binge-watching trashy TV shows. Yet we struggle to sustain positive habits like exercising regularly, meditating, spending time with friends and family, or connecting to nature – activities that we know nurture our body mind and soul.

Returning to the six aspects of personal power helps us to sustain our intentions. We need to find ways to rouse ourselves and activate our Motivation, Inspiration, Discipline, Big Picture, Compassion and Confidence. The key, once again, is Centering. Centering is how we reignite our personal power and return our power to its benevolent mode. Centering tames our dragon and builds our sense of Confidence.

 Lengthen your spine, soften your chest and expand to fill the room – smile.

While reading this book you have been centering many times. By centering repeatedly, you have been building a state of being that is resourceful and creative. You have been building a capacity to take action, to implement and sustain your intentions.

Take every opportunity to uplift, open up and connect to your bigger resourceful self. Relate to the part of you that is outside your skin and surrounds you. That part of you has access to great wisdom, Compassion and courage. When you think of inspiring people, places and things, you shift your perception of a situation and tap into your resourceful, Resilient self.

We need to constantly work with the elements of Personal Power – it is like swimming upstream; we must swim against the current of need and greed. Swimming upstream makes us strong and allows our wisdom and Compassion to shine through fears and irritations.

SOCIAL POWER

PERSONAL POWER

There are teachings that describe diamonds as a metaphor for finding our inner brilliance through spiritual practice. For the brilliance to shine the diamond has to be cut. Diamond cutting is the practice of changing a diamond from a rough stone into a faceted gem. The cut of a diamond greatly affects a diamond's brilliance; this means if it is cut poorly, it will be less luminous. The angle of the cut underneath is what makes the top of the diamond luminous.

In this metaphor, Personal Power is the foundation for Social Power. It is the base that allows Social Power to become benevolent, shiny and effective in the world. Developing our Personal Power skillfully is like having the right angle of the cut. This allows our Social Power skills to shine, creating positive influence and bringing inspiration to our endeavors.

When we *Center* we are cultivating openness and expansiveness. We are tapping into our benevolent dragon and inviting it to come through us. We are not making that happen – power is already happening - we open and let it flow through us. When we are able to implement and sustain, we begin to succeed in our endeavors. But that success can come with visibility and its challenging consequences.

Visibility

> *When we see power as a gift, we realize we are perpetually in the position to choose when and whether we will give and to whom—and whether to throw it away or invest it. We perceive anew our own capacity to shape how others respond to us, and thus our capacity to shape the world.*

—Eric Liu

If there was ever a time to step into the spotlight, to let yourself be seen and heard – this is it.

When we live in an empowered way that is influential and effective, we become visible. Our visibility coupled with a natural resistance to change can bring negative reactions from others. We will stand out and people will project their own desires and fears onto us. Given the power of homeostasis – the natural resistance to change – when we act in an empowered way we may receive negative reactions. If we change and begin to stand out, our relationships are likely to change; we might be subject to criticism, rumors or gossip that seems very far from our experience of what is true. How do we keep our balance and equanimity when we are in the unfamiliar territory of being visible and feel that the world around us is shifting?

When we are in the spotlight we can summon our benevolent dragon and draw upon our Motivation, Inspiration and Discipline. Calling on our personal power helps us reconnect to the Big Picture, Compassion and Confidence. There may be changes in the way friends or coworkers relate to us. They may want more of our time or look to us for positive feedback or compliments. We may find people are more critical and they may even make up stories that put us in a bad light.

To adapt to these changes we may need to forge new relationships or spend time in our own company. Supportive community is important to us as we continue our journey toward living up to our potential. It is important to recognize that community isn't always comprised of people. For St. Francis, community was animals and nature; for me the archetypes and deceased spiritual teachers are community as well as friends and family.

We can feel uncomfortable in our body when we are in the spotlight. Our mind might like the idea of standing out and when it actually happens, we might have a feeling of being self-conscious and overwhelmed. Our bodies anticipate this and manifest so much discomfort that we may decide to withdraw from the spotlight which means that we will not be able to make our full contribution. Being able to tolerate standing out is important if we want our voice to be heard. Shifting to our *centered* self and focusing on the part of us that is in the space around our bodies help us relax.

We can let whatever projections people have about us land in the space around us, not in our bodies. The space becomes a shock absorber for things people say and do. If the words don't land in us, if they land in the space, we don't have to take it all so personally; we can be more at ease and find some perspective.

 There are people who want you to succeed. Imagine that those people have their hands on your back, take a moment to feel the support. Remember we are all in this together.

This quick centering can help our benevolent dragon to emerge. We can stand in the spotlight knowing that we are acting on behalf of others, that we are serving a cause and encouraging others to find their passion and their voice.

Serving

I don't know what your destiny will be, but one thing I know: the only ones among you who will be really happy are those who have sought and found how to serve.

–Albert Schweitzer

As I became interested in exploring power, I read quite a few books on the subject. One of the themes that they all had in common was the tendency for 'absolute power to corrupt'.

Most of the literature points to two principles that can inhibit corruption. The first is to be sure that as your power increases you have friends or colleagues who will give you honest feedback so you can 'course correct.' It is hard to, 'read the label from inside the bottle' – in other words it can be difficult to see when we start slipping into a self-serving mode of behavior. The second principle is to be sure that you are working on behalf of others, not just creating gain for yourself. As the Albert Schweitzer quote points out, our soul is happiest when we are doing actions that help us all flourish.

Staying with your intentions to serve may also mean tolerating the projections and criticisms that will come even from people close to you. This is where spirituality comes in. Spirituality is defined as: "The quality of being concerned with the human spirit or soul as opposed to material or physical things." This has nothing to do with religion – I am referring to the positive feeling that arises when we are kind and considerate. When we are touched by a person's spirit, our heart opens; when we see someone smile, we want to smile. When we nourish our spirit and our soul and the spirit of others, we are being spiritual. We are connecting with our benevolent dragon.

When we are committed to doing things for other people, we find a sense of well-being and balance is needed. If we do not look after ourselves, we can't serve well. In the caregiving professions this is known as 'compassion burnout.' Getting enough sleep, eating well, exercising, and spending time with family and friends is crucial to cultivating a healthy lifestyle, and a healthy lifestyle allows us to have the energy to serve others.

 Inhale, lighten up, soften your chest as you exhale, relate the space around you. Think of an inspiring moment.

In his book, *Mandela's Way*, Richard Stengel says, "The Renaissance idea of individuation never penetrated Africa like it did Europe and America. The African model of leadership is better expressed as ubuntu, the idea that people are empowered by other people, we become our best selves through unselfish interaction with others." Centering rouses our benevolent dragon, and reminds us that we are in this together, helping us move from the me, to the we. Consider again this African proverb: 'If you want to go fast, go alone. If you want to go far, go together.'

It's Not an Easy Road

> *Always remember you have within you the strength, the patience and the passion to reach for the stars to change the world.*

–Harriet Tubman

The thing about power is that it is very attractive. People want to 'be with' those who are perceived as powerful. I have seen it over and over in my aikido career. Sadly the seductive nature of power often results in inappropriate relationships between students and teacher. I can see the temptation. It is all too easy for our sometimes-fragile ego to be seduced by adoration.

When we are courageous enough to summon our dragon power, we can expect the road will not be easy. Our lives will be filled with people who attribute their own fears and desires to us. They expect us to deliver more than we can deliver. They ask for favors and criticize us when we cannot give them what they want. There are those who expect us to fail and dismiss us when we do show a way forward.

Our benevolent dragon can help us to meet these challenges. We can be bigger than the naysayers and can meet their negativity with our positivity. Instead of tensing at criticism, we can open up and put the negative words and actions in the space in front of us, even in a bucket or a bowl where it can be examined at a distance. Not taking criticism personally allows our wisdom and compassion to surface. When people see us behave in this way, they want to invest in us and in our benevolent power.

 Inhale and uplift, exhale and soften, remember you are not alone, inspiration is all around you.

Power is currency, and with it you can procure goods and services, allegiance and support. How you use this currency is a reflection of your ability to make choices. This book is a suggestion, a reminder to be aware of how you gather, build and use your power currency. It is useful to remember that it is most helpful when it is used to serve a greater cause.

Take time every day to question your motivations. Are you acting because you want admiration and greater comfort? Or are you acting to bring more Compassion and equity into the world? Humility is a good way to counter our drive to be admired and discipline is a good counter for our drive for excess comfort.

Remind yourself who or what inspires you, commit to the Discipline of centering regularly, and consider the Big Picture. What might be the consequences in the future of your actions today? Take time to cultivate Compassion, and invite yourself to be courageous and confident.

Gestures of Power

In two famous studies on what makes us like or dislike
somebody, UCLA psychology professor Albert Mehrabian
created the 7-38-55 rule. That is, only 7 percent of a message
is based on the words while 38 percent comes from the tone
of voice and 55 percent from the speaker's body language
and face.
From the book, *Never Split the Difference*
— Voss, Chris; Raz, Tahl.

Notice what Dr. Mehrabian said: more than half of what
someone says comes across nonverbally. For me, 'body language
and face' means gestures.

In our Leadership Embodiment training, we often have people
from different countries who sometimes struggle with the
English language. We encourage them to take their partner
through the exercises in their native language. Some even
practice the exercises in silence, using only gestures, and the
information is communicated clearly.

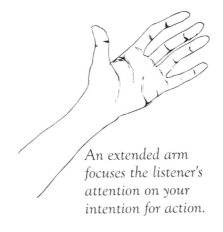

An extended arm
focuses the listener's
attention on your
intention for action.

Gestures of power can be
assertive or receptive. A
gesture can be assertive by
making a triangle shape:
extending your arm or
pointing with an extended
arm focuses the listener's
attention on your intention
for action.

On the other hand, letting the palms of your hands rest on your knees, the arms of the chair or the table while thinking of something that makes you smile is a receptive gesture, one of Warmth, openness and inclusion. Receptive gestures make people feel included and accepted. As a result, they can relax and be more open to what you are saying.

Receptive Gesture

A posture of dignity, an uplifted spine, is another gesture of power, one that communicates a feeling of Confidence. These kinds of gestures garner respect, and when there is mutual respect we can have more fruitful conversations. Disciplining ourselves not to slouch, close up, and contract is important if we want to have respect. We will need to show respect if we want to have a voice, keep conversations going, and forge relationships that will support contributions in the world.

Dragons and Power — the Adventure

Engaging with Dragons and Power is a daring and potentially dangerous adventure. In the martial arts traditions we often use weapons – generally wooden sticks and swords – to test our bravery and our ability. In this dragon adventure, Centering is our most powerful weapon. We use it to meet and match the challenge of our malevolent dragon. In Aikido we don't win over or beat our attacker. The most impressive principle in Aikido is that we 'protect the attacker'. When we *Center* we summon our protector dragon – the dragon that is willing to accept and protect its dark counterpart.

Centering helps us to become whole; like the yin yang symbol, the dark and the light together make the whole. When we become distracted and opt for security rather than generosity, we can use the weapon of centering to combat our selfishness.

When we *Center*, we have the potential to embody all aspects of our personal power. We are Motivated, Inspired, and Disciplined. We see the Big Picture and are Compassionate and Confident. Our benevolent dragon is energized and ready to engage. Our practice brings this dragon to life so that we can take courageous action and contribute. To embark on this adventure we need Size – our capacity to be expansive – Warmth, Resilience, Connection, Knowledge and Intuition. We have all that we need to train our dragon.

You can apply the centering practice and shift from 'me' to 'we'. When you *Center* you will look and feel different. You will have summoned your power dragon. By centering many times a day, you will begin to make an uplifted, open state your natural way of being. You will become who you are – a Noble, Awesome and Shiny person.

ACKNOWLEDGEMENTS

It has taken this book has been a few years to find its way to manifestation. As is usually the case with my books, there have been many false starts and it has been the same for this one. It is as if the Mystery invites me to explore a number of different possibilities before giving me a green light for a way forward. In that spirit I would like to thank and acknowledge the Mystery for its invitation to explore the deep reservoir of possibilities that can offer the world support for its evolving journey.

I am so grateful to Tiphani Palmer, my daughter, my partner, and my friend who has been a rock and a light throughout my process of meanderings and confusion before finding clarity. Thank you Mette Norgard for pushing me to find my authentic view on Power and for introducing me to my wonderful editor Janis Chan. Thank you Janis for your keen editing eye, your coaching and support. To Cian Geraghty thank you for your graphics and your patience with my many requests for changes. To Lynda Ray a deep bow of appreciation for taking on the final editing and jumping into the deep end of the publishing process – you never cease to amaze me with your willingness to learn new skills. To John Lund creative photographer with amazing patience and humor, thank you for the beautiful cover art.

Many thanks to Eileen Fisher, Greg Zelonka and Antoinette Klatzky for creating the platform and giving me the opportunity to begin to explore how we use our Power. Thank you to Paul Ciske, Brennan Culver, RJ Jennings, and Anjali Sawhney for your support with the LE classes that have been a laboratory to explore power over the years. The encouragement and kindness of the UK, EU community at the retreats helped me to continue my exploration – thank you to Amanda Ridings, Pierre Goirand, Anouk Brack and Paul King for being part of the unfolding. To my dear friends in Cape Town, South Africa - Karen White, Lisa Hansford, Ute Kuhlmann and Kerry Hammerton - many thanks for your continued support and for your warm hearts and bright spirits and your benevolent power.

To all the people who have taken courses and retreats over the past few years a deep bow of gratitude. Thank you for your willingness to explore this process and lend your voice and feedback – you have all helped shape the view of this book. May we all continue to be Noble, Awesome and Shiny.